If We Say It Enough We'll Believe It

Roger Hedgecock
and
Francine Phillips

If We Say It Enough We'll Believe It

Library of Congress Catalog Card Number: 92-62996
ISBN: 0-942259-07-6
Co-Edition by Westerfield Enterprises, Inc. and Write Now!

For information, contact
Write Now!
P.O. Box 3987
La Mesa, CA 91944-3987

Cover Design: The Art Ranch

Cover Art: Dan Pegoda

Typesetting: Artwerks

Printing: Vanard Lithographers

Printed in the United States of America

Table of Contents

PREFACE

Just So You Know

Early December, 1985. The phone call to the mayor's office was from Jim Price, general manager of KSDO AM 1130 NewsTalk Radio.

"If the worst happens – and I hope it doesn't – please consider doing a talk show for KSDO," said Jim.

I laughed and thanked him for the offer. Then the worst did happen. A clever concoction of politically motivated lies framed as an indictment by the District Attorney, propelled by the propaganda of The San Diego Union *and* The San Diego Tribune, *and given legitimacy in a kangaroo court where only one side was heard boosted into orbit as a jury verdict – guilty of 13 felonies!*

The mayor was the ex-mayor. I took my family to a remote beach in Baja and read Marcus Aurelius and grieved. Then I resolved to come back, make a fresh start and take up Jim Price's offer.

Two weeks later I came home and called Jim. "Do I still have the job?" I asked. He said yes. But it would be a year before he told me the whole story – the 14 duffel bags of negative mail, the editorial denunciation in the Union, *the loss of advertisers like Jack-in-the-Box and Dixieline Lumber. Jim Price had withstood the heaviest barrage of pressure anyone can imagine to keep his word to me.*

Seven years later, I'm still at KSDO. Better than that, my 9 a.m. to noon community forum consistently ranks first among all radio listeners in San Diego during that time period. More important still, by sharing my knowledge and experience with listeners, I've had the satisfaction of seeing ordinary people achieve extraordinary changes in San Diego.

Together, for example, we've fought and defeated an SDG&E rate increase, exposed the welfare fraud mess and the trouble at Child Protective Services, organized We The People, been members of DRIP and Light Up the Border. Talk has turned into action for the good of all of us. And that was why I went into politics in the first place. Thank you, San Diego, and thank you, Jim Price, for the opportunity.

And thank you to the California Supreme Court which, three years later, overturned the felony convictions because of, among other reasons, the discovery of jury tampering by the bailiff.

But this book is not about me or my trials. It's about you and the kind of San Diego you would like to pass on – and what you can do to achieve the great potential of this dream of a place we call home.

Roger Hedgecock
November, 1992

Just So You Understand

San Diego is a really interesting town. Compared to L.A. and Washington, D.C., living in San Diego is not complicated. The politics are pretty straightforward, the players are pretty recognizable. Since coming here ten years ago, it has been my observation that this is a place where a person can make a difference.

That has not been my only observation. From my perch as managing editor of The Wittenberg Door, *I was able to look behind the pulpits and get a feel for the religious life here. As editor of* San Diego Woman, *when it was in its fledgling stages, I had the opportunity to meet one-on-one with our city's most savvy and resourceful leaders – Diane Powers, Lynn Schenk, Billy Reilly, Marianne McDonald – and was able to interview the mayor, Roger Hedgecock. My stint as society editor for the* La Jolla Light *enabled me to observe closely and intimately the frolics of our most dignified business titans and the inner workings of the very wealthy. As managing editor for* The Daily Californian, *the relationship between the city and the county became clear as well as the stalemate of power that was bringing us to crisis.*

But you can only observe for so long. I started Write Now! to help people tell their stories, to enable people to finally start on that book or script that they've always wanted to write. But I needed to tell my own story first. When Roger and I joined forces, it was great to find out it was **our** *story. By talking to more and more people about our book, I'm finding that it is* **the** *story and that there are thousands of people in this town who want to take a good look San Diego, take a minute to laugh at our-*

selves, and then to move forward into the new century. You may love or hate this book. But if it can start a dialogue and get you to act, well, then the next story of San Diego will be your story, too.

Francine Phillips
November, 1992

"Never doubt that a small group of thoughtful, committed citizens can change the world; indeed, it's the only thing that ever has."

– Margaret Mead

1

The Great San Diego Booster Club

.

This City Is Not Supposed To Be Here

When Juan Rodriguez Cabrillo waded ashore here in 1592, he met a water-parched coastal desert, a small number of natives making a thirsty existence off small game, meager cultivation and occasional fishing. Buckwheat and cactus were the indigenous plants, with the occasional Torrey pine providing spotted shade. Cabrillo gathered his crew ashore, looked around and knew what he had to do. He made the priest perform a mass.

In all of its history, there have never been natural resources to sustain any type of industry at all in San Diego. No coal, no oil, no minerals. The gold mines of Julian provided a small flurry of riches that quickly played out. Until we developed specialty crops, there was no significant agriculture. Until Captain Medina invented the purse seine net, there was even precious little commercial fishing.

Normal sources of wealth, normal reasons for city growth in the 19th and early 20th Centuries simply did not exist here. Off the beaten path, in the southwest corner of the United States, San Diego was the ultimate cul de sac. There was no intrinsic value to San Diego at all.

Except for the vision of what could be. Father Junipero Serra was sent to the San Diego mission, the furthest outpost of the Catholic Church, with very little expectation. At that time, La Paz was the center of coastal life on the Baja peninsula and the remote region called Alta California was the Siberia of colonization and Church growth.

From the beginning, the problem was fresh water. So, the Padre immediately put Indian labor to good Christian use by building the

Mission Gorge Dam, portions of which are still visible. It was the first attempt to expand the water supply in San Diego. Since then, every generation has strived to expand and control water – up to and including our own. Today the sun glistening on a snow-covered slope in Colorado provides water out of a tap in Clairemont. The poetic journey of a single drop of water has very little to do with cosmic consciousness and a whole lot to do with power, money and development of land. Without imported water, San Diego could not exist.

The Great Booster Club

Because there is no inherent reason for San Diego - no natural purpose for our existence - we are open and eager to follow the whims of someone who will define us in more concrete terms. Let's be this! is the cry of the visionary, the result of the latest government-sponsored study, the demand of the wealthiest land developer. And with a Mickey Rooney/Judy Garland optimism, we put on the show.

Over the decades we were a trading outpost, then a health mecca, then a Navy town, then a tourist town, then a tourist city, then an international trade center, then a biotech town. Finally, as a mix of all of the above, we have become "America's Finest City." If we say it enough, we'll believe it.

Back in the early development of the area, Alonzo Horton battled the city council over the location of the city. We had San Diego (Old Town) and we had New Town – squares of scrublands being divided and sold as city blocks. Horton's vision of the importance of the waterfront took years to achieve. It took, in fact, a booster club of land speculators and developers declaring the strip the city center.

A little while later, the San Diego Boosters had a vision of our town being the gateway to the Panama Canal. The 1915 Panama-California Exposition was held in glorious Balboa Park created by the vision of Kate Sessions. Still later, the airport was taking off, as T. Claude Ryan was trying to scrape together biplanes and earn the money to build the plane for Lindbergh's historic flight to France. Mission Bay was the vision of a small group, inspired by City Engineer Glenn Rick, who saw the possibilities available in dredging the swampy muck and creating a water playground for San Diego residents and the world. The stadium was built through the single-mindedness of Jack Murphy and a group of downtown business boosters. This amazing group sold 72% of the voters on the idea that we should spend $27 million that we didn't have, to build a stadium on a bean field in a river bottom. For teams that weren't there.

Pete Wilson's holy grail became downtown redevelopment. Horton Plaza fulfilled part of Ernie Hahn's vision for San Diego and he was smart enough to insist that the Convention Center be included as a keystone to downtown redevelopment. The Booster Club went into high gear in 1984 to get voter approval for Roger's vision of a Convention Center on the waterfront paid for in cash by the Port Commission.

Who Will Be Our Champion?

Our history contains layer after layer of shifting coalitions gath-

4

ered around strong individuals who have tried, and are still trying, to define San Diego. The amazing thing is that it works at all. In fact, some of the wackiest ideas defining our town have actually turned out to be O.K. while the most studied and thought out projects have been failures. In a town with a largely military mentality, a hero leading battalions is a model that works.

C. Arnholt Smith was probably the closest person San Diego ever had to a town boss. Smith owned the bank, owned the Padres and pretty much owned the town. He had most of the action and, for many years, reigned unchallenged. He approved the politicians and approved the loans. But Smith did not have the impact or the long-lasting legacy of the Rockefellers of New York or Walter Beech of Kansas City. His downfall was sudden.

In 1970, Smith backed the wrong candidate for district attorney. Backed by Richard Silberman and Robert Peterson, Ed Miller, who is still San Diego's district attorney, won that election. Shortly thereafter Miller set into motion the destruction of Smith's control. Eventually, Smith was indicted, convicted and discredited, his leadership suddenly gone.

Because the paradox of San Diego is that as much as we call for leaders, for heroes, and accomplish nothing without them, we are a city that loves, as well, to bring a hero to his knees. There is a nasty streak in the San Diego mentality that likes nothing better than to expose the clay feet of the icons we create. Nothing affirms the collective lack of self-esteem more quickly. If San Diego created it, it just can't be that great.

And this rise and fall, this boosterism mixed with cynicism has

5

brought us to the San Diego of today. Paralyzed, incapable of decisive action, surrounded by contradictions that demand definition. Who are we? Who is in charge? Who will put a new vision before us?

The lack of a hero spells obvious confusion. As new waves of immigrants take up residency, the population is bulging in new directions, with new definitions for our town. The coalitions are getting smaller, more numerous and more contradictory. The visions are beginning to clash. We are still creating a San Diego that isn't here, but we're just not sure where it is. Who we are. Who we should be.

"I'd like to see the government get out of war altogether and leave the whole feud to private industry."

– Joseph Heller

2

The Military/Industrial/ Educational Marriage

If the Japanese had not bombed Pearl Harbor on December 7, 1941, San Diego would probably have remained an out-of-the-way resort town with its only claim to higher learning a small teachers' college on Normal Street. Both war and education have had tremendously positive impacts on our town. After Pearl Harbor, San Diego's strategic location and natural harbor lured military leadership to our shores.

The entrepreneurs of the day, through sheer will power and determination, built huge industries to keep the war machine well-oiled and efficient. San Diego became an example of the military/industrial complex in its most pure form - rationally planned, government financed and locally implemented. Never mind that the citizens of San Diego were archly conservative and determined to get the government off their backs and out of their pockets. Never mind that the heroic ideal has always been the individual fighter, the lone aviator and the entrepreneur. Never mind the fact that that same entrepreneur is completely financed by the government. If we can maintain our illusion of autonomy, we're O.K. If we don't say it, no one will think of it.

So this joint partnership between private industry and military spending got San Diego off to a great start during World War II. And after the war, it was only natural to extend this same process to education. The G.I. bill was born. The G.I. bill prompted hundreds of thousands of young men and women to get higher education. They had earned it. It was free. Why not? The G.I. bill was basically a voucher system, hugely successful because it allowed veterans to choose their own education - trade schools, religious schools or academic institutions.

As a result, San Diego was flooded with students and we accommodated their needs. San Diego State College flourished on Montezuma Mesa and eventually, through the persuasive efforts of Dr. Roger Revelle, UCSD was founded in La Jolla on an unused military base. Along the way we developed the Community College system, and picked up a variety of other educational institutions, such as USD, Point Loma Nazarene College and USIU. No less than five law schools teach the finer points of legal practice. Higher learning funded by the G.I. bill and later, the student loan program.

So San Diego transformed the military/industrial marriage into a military/educational/industrial family.

The Real Curriculum

The real money in education after WWII came from the interwoven goals of war preparation, technological research, scientific exploration and improving bright young minds to take military and commercial advantage of all this new knowledge. And they did. Young engineers shot out of World War II with all of the military contacts, furthered their education and used government contracts to build companies. The spin-offs from military research were commercially developed and what evolved were multi-billion dollar businesses, run after the pattern of the defense establishment.

Time after time, company after company, San Diego has been built with the blessings and the underwriting of the military. And the military benefitted as well. San Diego minds perfected the Tomahawk cruise missile, the Stealth Bomber and the SDI technology. Followers of James Bond have always been convinced that laser beams could be effective weapons, but it took a group of San Diego engineers to prove it.

Meanwhile, the educational institutions have been built with CIA grants, Pentagon grants and NASA grants. We have built beautiful and advanced laboratories on our university campuses and our beaches and sunshine have guaranteed that our faculty rosters included the best in the nation, the most select in the world. Our work force has been the most educated in the country and that, in turn, has brought more business to town. These businesses, in their turn, built beautiful and advanced products with the best and most select personnel in the world.

For more than forty years and through three generations, this family cohesion binding government, industry and education has worked like a dream. But we're heading toward divorce. The 1990s have found San Diego again being impacted by war and education. Except this time there is no war and we are dismantling education. The funding is running out and we have to make some budget cuts. Where are they going to be made?

Physics, chemistry, German, Russian, aerospace engineering. The budget cuts proposed in 1992 by President Tom Day at San Diego State University are directly dismantling the structure that has created jobs and prosperity in San Diego since World War II. It is not just that those classes are cancelled and those types of students will be else-where, but San Diego will not have the talent in the work force that can keep the desired industries intact and in town.

For instance, the aerospace laboratory at SDSU has done materials and process testing for every aerospace engineering firm in San Diego, creating close business ties and offering our students a leg up in getting hired on as engineers. This effective relationship will end if the department closes and can the departure of every aerospace company, not only General Dynamics, be too far behind?

Another example of the military/education/industry formula has been the development and prominence of the biotech industry in San Diego.

The biotech industry got its start in San Diego like other industries — government research grants paid for basic research. The findings from the research resulted in scientific patents. The patents caused spin-off industries to develop. And dedicated, single-minded researchers who, everybody thought, had their noses in their Bunsen burners, turned out to be very savvy entrepreneurs and got rich. Enough of these entrepreneurs spun off enough successful businesses for San Diegans to take notice.

But a funny thing happened on the way to our new prosperity because of the United States budget deficit. The funding for disease control is on the decline. The cure for diabetes and the need for a new heart valve is important, but not a matter of national security. And biotech firms that have been involved with national security issues, such as biological warfare and genetic engineering were caught short by the end of the Cold War. Then the use of aborted fetuses got involved. Then animal rights activists had their say. Then the hazardous waste issue came up.

The biotech firms started the Biotechnical Industry Roundtable, led by David Hale of Gensia Pharmaceuticals, and told San Diego leadership that they had better take a long, hard look at the obstacle course they were erecting against the industry. Now biology is being cut back in SDSU's curriculum.We are at a crossroads with education. War, as a stimulant for investment, is fading. We can't allow education to follow suit. Is there a way to continue this link with the government, to keep this cycle intact?

One of the new funding sources for education is industry itself. American businesses are spending more dollars on education and training than ever before. There is a far greater desire to keep an employee and upgrade his knowledge than to continue to recruit the youngest and brightest each year.

Mass adoption of the Continuous Improvement model for industry has required not just performance retraining, but an entire retraining of the mind set of workers. Psychological testing, drug testing, personality typing, efficiency training, stress workshops, time management. The corporation has become the post-graduate educational institution and it's being paid for by higher consumer prices rather than higher income and property taxes.

Every Room a Classroom

Private alternatives are also filling the gap, subsidized by industry. National University was a harebrained idea that wasn't given much of a chance when David Chigos started it in the '70s. Now there are hundreds of courses of study and several campuses. The Learning Annex has proliferated and been copied throughout the U.S. The Center for Professional Studies is a new San Diego institution and we have a hotel that is devoted entirely to seminars and workshops. San Diego offers thousands of additional avenues each and every day for corporate training, from management by yoga to getting ahead by being obnoxious. You want to learn it, God knows there's an expert in San Diego willing to teach a class in it. We can all be students forever.

In the meantime, however, we may be destroying education for the next generation. It's too costly. It's intimidating. Parents can't pay for it anymore and, really, does it make a difference? There are waiters and cab drivers here with Ph.D.s, so where does it get them? The link between education and the economy is primary and San Diego is letting that link slip away. It could be our most tragic bungling of all.

Because, even though the corporation as teacher/trainer model may be providing some learning, corporate-induced personality and/or morality will never take the place of the free exchange of ideas, the training of critical thinking and the plain old interaction with information that our higher educational institutions have offered all minds, young and old, for the last 40 years.

Build the Library

Whatever we do about education, San Diego simply must have a new library.

And I don't mean a building. In fact, if we stop thinking about the building as a depository of books and starting thinking about it as an information center, the old central library is probably suitable and could be renovated.

Dale Carnegie built the first library system in 1908 with the understanding that people would come to America and learn the culture, study our history and get free access to information about what it means to be an American. Information was the basic building block of a democratic society and it was the government's duty to provide that information to its citizens. It was the building block of American society.

It still makes sense. How can we use the technology available, or create new technology to make a library for the future? Is there a way to link the libraries of our universities, our medical school, our law schools and our communities? Can we make terminals available to the public? Can we create a center for learning English, learning to type, learning to use computers?

Information access is still the building block of a free society. It is still the priority need for creating an educated, informed and productive population. If San Diego's future lies in research, learning and education, we need to stop debating about a building and make available the information technology of tomorrow, today.

If San Diego is going to continue to grow heroes, continue to set the stage for the individual leaders that have created this city from nothing, and regain the confidence that we have lost as a region, we need to be able to think, read, write and express ourselves with sophistication. It may not really matter whether that happens through night courses, corporate seminars, audiotapes from the new library or computer modem classes. It just **has** to happen.

"Nothing will ever be attempted if all possible objections must first be overcome."

– Dr. Samuel Johnson

3

Getting Off The Ground

The aerospace industry, so important to San Diego and now so endangered, is an outgrowth of the fascination with transportation on the part of our city's early heroes. The reasoning for this fascination is simple. Without people coming and going, in some form or another, we would have no economy.

The Western Terminus Of Somewhere

In the 1880s San Diego was intent on becoming the western terminus of the Union Pacific Railroad. If we had had our way, New York tycoons, Chicago hit men and Texas oil barons would have stepped into the sunshine for their first breath of California air in National City.

At the time San Diego and Los Angeles were about the same size and there seemed every reason to bring the rail here. The Union Pacific Railroad, however, didn't agree. They gave their western terminus to L.A. and that fact determined for all time that Los Angeles would become the major city on the West Coast. In 1915 we sought to become the terminus for all travel through the Panama Canal. San Diego citizens passed a $2 million bond issue to stage the legendary Panama-California Exposition creating Balboa Park out of hard dirt and built temporary structures that would display the permanence of our commitment to a West Coast port of entry for the Panama trade. That didn't work either. Los Angeles again beat us, even though we had a spectacular natural harbor and L.A.'s harbor was completely artificial.

Then came aviation. The Navy was the first step. Because of our wonderful climate, the Navy has, from almost the beginning of flight, had a field at North Island. Following World War I, San Diego became a very active center for pilots, aviation training and, later, aircraft factories. Reuben Fleet brought his Consolidated Aircraft Company from Buffalo, New York, to San Diego.

Fleet and T. Claude Ryan along with other aviation pioneers formed the nucleus of a manufacturing base built almost exclusively on government contracts. Small airports dotted the county, all pointing to the possibility of a major aviation center. Together, these aviators built Lindbergh Field. The airport.

Lindbergh Field was created in 1929 out of a dredged portion of San Diego Bay. It was the largest civic project ever attempted by the citizens of San Diego up to that time and was a tremendous accomplishment. At its completion, it became the most easily accessed airport in the United States. Which would have been great, except there were no air carriers coming into San Diego at the time. Like many other San Diego civic projects, such as the stadium and the convention center, it was built before we quite knew what to do with it. If you build it, they will come.

And come they did. As San Diego went into World War II, the population started jumping by nearly 10,000 people each month. Lindbergh Field had round the clock use. When J. Floyd Andrews started Pacific Southwest Airlines after the war, it was the heyday for the airport.

Transportation found a home. Andrews vision for PSA was not only to fly to L.A. and San Francisco, but to link all of California. Small towns like Fresno, San Jose, Sacramento and Santa Barbara would be networked into a travel pattern that would allow Californians to be mobilized. He took a bunch of DC3's from the war, painted them orange and began his airline.

At the beginning, the stewardesses wore long skirts and tailored, Eisenhower-type jackets. As the idea took off and California gained its baby-boom reputation for fun, the planes wore smiles and the stewardesses wore hot pants. It was a heyday all right.

Meanwhile, dozens of other cities in the United States were beginning the debate about airport locations. Would a small, convenient city airport be sufficient to meet the needs of the future? Most of these cities concluded it would not. In the '50s and '60s, cities like Chicago, New York, Washington, D.C. and Dallas built very large airports outside of their city limits. They were building their "next generation" airports, utilizing thousands of acres. San Diego never did.

Lindbergh Field does not have the terminal space, the parking space, the runway space or the acreage to be an international airport. The Phoenix airport sits on 15,000 acres. The new, "third generation" airport in Denver broke ground on 126,000 acres. Lindbergh Field has 490 acres. What shall we do?

The Studies

The first study that concluded the airport to be noisy, overcrowded and dangerous was in 1945. It recommended several changes, including location. As one result, the terminal was moved from the corner of Pacific Coast Highway and Laurel Street to Harbor Drive.

Airport studies came thick and fast after that. Everybody – the Chamber of Commerce, the county, the city and even the Port, when it inherited the airport in the early '60s, began to study the airport. There have been 34 studies in the last 30 years.

More Studies

By 1968, something called the Comprehensive Planning Organization (CPO) was born in response to the rapid growth in San Diego that, at the same time, was causing division and decentralization of the power. Lots of individual cities were incorporating and communities were beginning to disassociate from the center of San Diego.

Dick Huff became the first executive director of the CPO whose purpose was to join cities together for planning purposes and to be a vehicle for voluntary association among the various local governments.

But the timing was wrong. CPO was viewed by many as a federal plot, designed to take over local government and to allow the feds to control our lives. With help from Congress, that's actually turned out to be half true. But by the early '70s the successor to this organization, SANDAG (San Diego Association of Governments), was determined to get an overview of the county to plan for systems and resource-use. SANDAG looked at all kinds of regional issues – transportation, land use planning, pollution control, sewage and waste. And the airport.

In 1974, the SANDAG airport study captured the attention of the new mayor, Pete Wilson, who strongly supported the idea of a large regional airport and the creation of a large San Diego. He did a study, too. And the best thinking of 1973-1974 agreed – a new regional airport should be built on Otay Mesa.

But this time the boosters balked. Otay Mesa was not a part of the City of San Diego at the time, so Wilson had to deal with the county and the county didn't want it there. The city also had problems with the airport being so close to Mexico, creating all kinds of fears about immigration, drug-smuggling and language problems.

So Pete Wilson got shot down. Otay Mesa was out. But everyone was convinced that there had to be an answer out there, so everyone set out to find it.

And More Studies

We studied a desert airport, with a huge tube running through the mountains. We studied an offshore floating airport, because so many of the pilots had aircraft carrier experience they didn't think it would be a problem to land in a small dot on the ocean.

North Island was considered. Miramar was considered. Palomar. Sorrento Valley. In all, 16 separate sites have been examined in detail and millions of dollars have been spent.

Meanwhile, the Port, which inherited the airport and all the other tidelands of San Diego Bay at its creation in 1963, quietly expanded it and has run it so efficiently, that the airport has become the goose that lays the golden egg. The Port District has made a fortune from the airport. So much, in fact, that although the Port has the authority to levy property taxes to pay for harbor improvements, it has never taxed anyone a penny. It has lived, and lived quite well, on the leases and fees and revenue produced by Lindbergh Field and other development on the harbor front.

And this fortune has served the community well. Because of the wealth of the Port District, they were able to build the Convention Center with $160 million. In cash. They are developing a cruise industry. They are expanding the embarcadero. They might even build a library.

Moving the airport would upset the whole relationship of money and power in San Diego. Who will run it? If it's not on the waterfront, the Port will lose it. Or will they? Maybe the Port should run it on Otay Mesa? Maybe we should study the feasibility of that?

If We Build It, Will We Really Want It?

Lindbergh Field is a metaphor for growth in San Diego. In the 1920s, it proved that we were right up there with other expanding, first-class cities. San Diego had looked ahead, taken a risk and succeeded in that risk. The city boomed. The airport was packed. We did good. So good, in fact, that while other cities looked ahead to the next generation of airports, we rested on the laurels of our pretty little convenient airport that made money.

But all along, San Diego has been determined to be "world class." The boosters have supported a great big convention center, a great big trolley line, great big hotels and condos downtown and are now considering a great big sports arena, city hall and library. The assumption has always been that we needed a great big airport as well. And the lack of airport expansion has been the one great step left and it is the one step that San Diegans have been absolutely unable to take.

By 1991 we had come full circle. Maureen O'Connor and Ron Roberts flew to Mexico City and tried to get the Mexican government interested again in the new version of the Otay Mesa airport, with new demographic studies. If you look at the population from Oceanside to Ensenada, Otay Mesa is dead center. Roberts vision looked at the reality that Mexico has come a long way since 1974.

At that time the population of Tijuana was half of San Diego's, many of them living in cardboard shacks. Now, Tijuana is larger than San Diego and billions of dollars and millions of people are crossing the border each year, legally and illegally, making our economies increasingly interdependent.

But there are very many people in San Diego that do not like that reality and these people attacked Otay Mesa airport with all their heart. Again the boosters balked. Ron Roberts failed. And it became clear that another community leader had stubbed his toe – and lost an election—by supporting something that was beyond the capacity of the majority of San Diegans to get excited about.

So this dilemma continues to confound San Diego. How can you be a big, international city without a big international airport? Of all the things that San Diego has wanted to be, an international center is certainly one of them. But do we still want to be big? The answer seems to be coming more and more clearly. No.

San Diego has reached a fork in the road and somewhere between the sewer spill, the America's Cup and the drought we seem to have chosen a path. Suppose (say an increasing chorus of voices) we become a less-than-big international city. Suppose we become a really important, small, international city. Well-known and respected, still cutting edge, still unique. But not overpopulated, not overrun, not all things to all people, not growing ever-larger. In short, not L.A.

The airport is still a metaphor and the metaphor is now this: If we don't build it they won't come.

How does this future sound?

Lindbergh Field can stay where it is. International flights and long-range flights will not fly directly in, and San Diegans can probably not fly directly out, but regional flights will abound. Shuttles to L.A. will have to do. Except for one thing. Tijuana *does* want to become a big international city.

The Mexican government wants Tijuana to become the western terminus to trade in Asia. Sound familiar? The difference is, they will succeed. By the end of the century, Tijuana will be far larger than San Diego and the industrialization of Baja will make our industrial parks look like boutiques. The maquiladoras are only the first step. Rodriguez Airport at Otay Mesa already has a Japanese Airlines repair facility and a runway to accept international flights. All it needs is a terminal, parking and customs facilities in the United States to complete its vision. This would make Rodriguez an airport accessible to Americans, but still under the operational control of Mexico. And Mexico is poised internationally to pull it off.

Where does this leave San Diego? It's possible that San Diego will become more of an elite city – where the bosses live. As manufacturing moves to Mexico there will not be the thousands of workers here except in service industries. We are going to become more managerial and professional, more high-tech and scientific. The financial institutions will regain their strength with education and research becoming our primary endeavors. This might be a very offensive scenario to a great many people. But it is also the most likely one to happen.

And the airport, finally, remains the metaphor for the kind of San Diego we want. Let Mexico run planes, deal with the air carriers, build the runways and make it all happen on time. San Diego will run a parking lot and a terminal and have access to international flights without depending on Los Angeles. And we won't have to ever study Lindbergh Field again and we can stay smaller and protected. Export the problems and keep the benefits. Meanwhile, back at San Diego Harbor.

A Real Port At Last?

The natural harbor is San Diego's greatest natural asset. The Navy, shipbuilders, fishermen and tourists use it to great advantage. But the Port of San Diego has never been a commercial trading center like the Port of L.A. – the point of trade for imports and exports for this whole part of the world. With the rise of Mexican industry in Tijuana, the Port has a new shot at the trade business. We have a container crane (virtually unused since its installation in 1972), we have the pier space, the storage space and the transportation to offer the maquiladora industries what they increasingly need. Yet we are still not going after this business with its tremendous opportunity for high-paying waterfront jobs.

So great is the need for port services, the Mexican government is investing millions of dollars to upgrade the Port of Ensenada to supply the maquiladoras and to offer a gateway for export of their products. Will another man-made port with inferior facilities rob San Diego of this income? L.A. did it to San Diego years ago, will Ensenada do it now? Where are the leaders who will step into this growing gap? If you snooze, you lose!

"America lives in the heart of every man everywhere who wishes to find a region where he will be free to work out his destiny as he chooses."

– Woodrow Wilson

4

Ollie Ollie Oxen In Free

San Diego and Tijuana are like non-identical twins that have been separated at birth. They hold a common heritage – products of the expansion of the Spanish Empire and the Mexican Revolution. The basic DNA components are the same — terrific weather, long stretches of gorgeous shore, clear skies, gentle breezes. There is even the same dearth of natural resources that have made them both dig in and create reasons to be cities. In fact, Tijuana is actually more of a man-made entity than San Diego.

But they've been raised in different households. San Diego's adopted parents are wealthy, English-speaking and part of the American empire. Tijuana, on the other hand, suffered from neglect and two foster parents — a judicial system that concludes you are guilty until proven innocent and a political system that is notoriously corrupt. The largest cultural influences have been Spanish and a little French. Ironically, given this background, Tijuana today has become hard-driving and entrepreneurial, while San Diego has had a tendency to merely whine.

The twins have grown up and become forcibly reunited and are eyeing each other warily and hungrily. It's a unique situation. Nowhere else in the world are first world and third world communities so closely juxtaposed. No other chasm between lifestyles is more radical than here. And the border, as barrier, has become a passageway.

You Say Penny, I Say Peso

Our two economies have now become tremendously intertwined.

San Diego's retail shopping centers depend vitally on Mexican shoppers. Mexico's industrial plants depend vitally on investments from American firms. There are Americans living in Tijuana and Mexicans living in San Diego. Each day there are thousands of examples, both legal and illegal, of the interaction between our two peoples.

At San Ysidro, the border has become the busiest, most frequently crossed border in the world. Thousands of people cross over it every day, with family, social, and industrial interests on both sides. American houses are filled with Mexican tile, Mexican light fixtures and Mexican-made furniture. Meanwhile when a house gets torn down in San Diego, Tijuana contractors cross the border to salvage the construction materials – so the same house can be rebuilt on Mexican soil. In a very real way, the border does not exist and never has.

But even if the physical fences built between the two cities are fairly recent, the mental barriers are deep-rooted. Both cities are protective of their cultural identities and have deep suspicions regarding the other. These differences can get bizarre. A few years ago Mexico City looked at the traffic in Tijuana and decided it was far too Americanized. So they made a decree – there will be no right turns on a red light. We don't do that in Mexico! And if you've ever turned right on a red light in Tijuana, you've gotten a swift lesson in cultural protectionism. And political corruption, for that matter.

San Diegans are also protective of cultural identity. The English-only initiative reflects the demand that Hispanics in this country are expected to adopt our culture, not adapt it. The fact that school graduation ceremonies in the border town of San Ysidro are conducted in

Spanish mocks the thousands of tax dollars spent on bilingual education and angers citizens who expect those given high school diplomas in the United States to be able to speak English.

But aside from the cultural encroachment that is causing emotional reactions ranging from discomfort to rage on the part of many San Diegans, and aside from the legal, political and policy-making apparatuses that have been created to deal with the friction caused by the diversity of the population, one myth persists: illegal immigration into the United States benefits our economy.

Or does it? Richard Parker and Louis Rea, both Ph.D.'s from San Diego State University, completed and presented to the California state legislature in July of 1992, the first study of the fiscal impact of the illegal immigration on San Diego County. The first. Ever.

What's It Costing Us?

The bottom line is that Parker and Rea estimate a *net* $146 million cost *each year* by San Diego County taxpayers for illegal immigrants. The bulk of it, more than $100 million, is spent in the criminal justice system. These arrests, arraignments and prison terms cost San Diego taxpayers, not the federal government. Not to mention the cost of a formal interpreter required at every trial.

The irony is that, according to some San Diego judges, the illegals are given preferential treatment for the most part and moved to a "fast track" system. After all, why give an illegal a long prison term, tying up jail space, when the sooner they are out the sooner they will be deported?

So illegal aliens are given quick service and short terms. Then, if all goes according to plan, they are formally charged by the federal government and deported to Mexico, never to be seen or heard from again. Crossing the border itself becomes a federal offense and we don't have to wait for them to commit a crime in San Diego to be apprehended.

But, that's where it breaks down. Because the federal government doesn't want to take the time to sue for formal deportation. What they do is ask for voluntary deportation. And when there is voluntary deportation the group of former inmates are rounded up, taken to the border and dropped off, where they can scatter and make their way back north. There is no local law against illegal immigration. The federal government is winking and we are paying.

So even though more than 50,000 illegal immigrants are apprehended and deported each month, thousands more coming through. The border patrol has its hands full weeding out the worst of the drug smugglers and the most inhumane of the immigrant smugglers. What happens when they get to San Diego? For many illegal immigrants, its only the first stop in a journey through social service agencies that extends north through Los Angeles, through the San Joaquin Valley and even to agricultural areas in the Midwest.

For others, estimated at 200,000, San Diego becomes home. About 9% of the population is believed to be undocumented, illegal residents. A large portion of these families are working, contributing to the tax base paying for health care and contributing to San Diego. Parker and Rea found the fiscal benefit of immigration to be close to $60 million per year. This is not new.

In 1979, Roger, a member of the County Board of Supervisors at the time, urged the County to do a landmark study. The study estimated the benefits of illegal immigrants residing here. There was a general sentiment that Mexican workers took jobs that Americans would not do, that the cheap, under-the-table labor they provided made for greener lawns, happier babies and generally lower prices for all San Diego manufacturing costs, not to mention the price of a good meal.

But in today's recessionary times, those benefits have been far outweighed by the fact that illegal immigrants have become a threat. In a time of cutbacks, spending $13 million dollars each year on social services for illegals begins to grate. $40 million spent by our strapped educational system seems unfair. Basic survival instincts are coming into to play here and the tension is building and may become an explosion.

The twist to all of this is that those most threatened by illegal immigration are the lower paid U.S. citizens, including Mexican-Americans. For example, this is happening in construction, where Mexican-Americans have traditionally been able to make good living.

At the time of this writing, the drywall workers are on strike. A few years ago drywallers were making 18 cents a square foot. Legal immigrants got a foothold in the industry and drove down the price. Now these same immigrants are striking to get four cents a foot, a price that is being undercut still further by illegals. So the tension mounts.

But even more disturbing than the illegals who take jobs away from citizens are the illegals who come and can't get jobs. There is no longer an open market for work here. Hundreds come and find that they cannot get jobs. They don't have money. They don't have food. And we are now seeing the fallout of an economy so strapped that the bottom rung is desperate. So we find them stealing cars, getting involved in drug deals and coming up with all kinds of survival techniques and schemes, such as the scam uncovered that used illegals as human decoys to cause highway accidents for the insurance money. It's starting to get ugly. People are getting mad.

And it is these feelings of threat, of fear and of anger, that are being totally ignored by the federal government. It is a fatal flaw of our foreign policy that the feelings produced by this proximity to the border are not being addressed. Not even acknowledged.

Light Up the Border

Muriel Watson is a widow living in Spring Valley. Her husband had been a border patrol agent and Muriel was well aware of the tension and disruption that illegal immigration can cause.

By 1989, Muriel had become dismayed by the stories of violence and horror that seemed to be growing daily. Children were abandoned; illegals were locked in cars and left to die. Not only was the border becoming increasingly dangerous to the Americans, it was becoming a site of terror for Mexicans as well. Muriel devised a plan.

She called Roger's show one morning and said, "I'm going down there, Roger. It's dark, its dangerous, people are getting hurt. I'm going to just park my car next to the Tijuana River and shine my head-lights on the border area. It may not do much, but it may do some-thing." Roger thought this was great and wished her well.

Soon Muriel called again.

"I'm going again, Roger," said Muriel. "This time there will be fif-teen of us going and we're all going to shine our lights." Roger cheered her on.

Muriel called again. "I've decided, Roger, that this is so important, so basic and so vital that I'm going to keep going until the federal gov-ernment puts up lights," said Muriel.

Roger was inspired and blurted out on the air, "Muriel, I'm going to be there, too. Give us directions." Light Up the Border switched on.

More than 1,500 people arrived at the Tijuana River bed that week-end. Light streamed across the barren sand as thousands of families were huddled with their bundles and their children to make the cross-ing. The Americans were from all races, backgrounds and walks of life, from conservative yuppies to radicalized elders, each with their own reason to be there. Each shining a beacon into the heart of the immigration problem.

The Hispanic activists went crazy. Roberto Martinez denounced the movement as racist and all the media in Tijuana took off with screaming headlines. Bob Burgreen, the San Diego chief of police, made a speech at a Tijuana country club denouncing Roger personally and labeling Muriel's supporters as racists as well.

It's interesting to note that at the same time this was happening, Mexico was rushing thousands of border guards south to seal off its border with Guatemala, where a civil war had produced thousands of illegals moving from Central America into Mexico. No word on border lights at that end.

But the next weekend's Light Up the Border campaign was met by hundreds of Mexican nationals carrying cardboard and foil reflectors meant to send back the light. This time they played their hand too far, however. Carrying anti-American signs and shouting that Californian belonged to them, it was an ugly display of political action and convinced many that the wave of illegal immigration was no less than a purposeful invasion of the United States.

Suddenly public opinion and official support swelled. Congressman Duncan Hunter convinced the National Guard to build a more permanent fence. Then, not to be left out, the Army Corps of Engineers declared that they would, indeed, put up lights. Federal policy was pushed into action by the determination of a Spring Valley widow. Because of the support of Roger and his listeners, the politics at the border have been changed for all time. Muriel Watson demonstrated for all of us again what one determined person can accomplish. She had the courage to address what NAFTA has ignored.

NAFTA Will Fix It

The North American Free Trade Agreement is a document long overdue in terms of boosting Mexico out of its feudal mentality and into the global free market. A great deal of good can come from this. A great deal of good already has. San Diegans make money, everyday, because we are close to Mexico. Mexicans make money, everyday, because they are close to San Diego. More trade will be good for both countries.

But you can't leave out the single most upsetting and threatening aspect of this relationship when you are crafting an agreement between nations. The NAFTA proposal says nothing about illegal immigration. Not a word. And after years and years of trying to get our federal government to understand the border situation, NAFTA makes one thing very clear. They just don't get it.

NAFTA was drafted to deal with trade. Then it was expanded to include some environmental issues. Then the Mexican government made demands regarding the core economics, maintaining sovereignty and other issues. It was an historic opportunity to negotiate our own demands on them – end illegal immigration. But the U.S. made no requests. All of the Mexican concerns were addressed. Ours were not acknowledged. It was an opportunity missed and the people of San Diego know it.

As a consequence, putting an end to illegal immigration is a huge problem without an answer that may become very explosive in the next few years. The drywall strikes are only the beginning.

Mexicans will continue to import their culture to our city as they come. Which is fine if you're talking about art and dance and restaurants. But if you are talking about labor relations, where gunfire is O.K. and sweatshop conditions are normal, there are going to be some strained situations.

The biggest challenge for our federal government is to say "Yes" to free trade and "No" to illegal immigration. It must say to Mexico, We respect your laws, your culture and your sovereignty. You must respect ours. And then it must put up a real fence, use the lights, enforce the law that makes it a crime to enter the United States illegally. Or, if Congress really wants these immigrants, be honest about it, change the law and let them legally come in.

"A little inaccuracy sometimes saves tons of explanation."

– H. H. Munro

5

Trashed

The rapid growth of San Diego County in the last 20 years has challenged our ability to anticipate the need for and to organize the funds to build a myriad of necessary services. Nowhere do we need leadership more than in the areas of sewage and waste. Some exemplary small businesses in San Diego are trying to explore new options, but as yet, no heroes have emerged from the heap.

Sewage - Caught In a Quagmire

In 1950, San Diego Bay was brown. It looked like, well, it looked like what was making it brown. And every day millions of gallons more of what was making it brown was being dumped into the bay.

Actually, the sewage was, at that time, being semi-treated. San Diego had built a WPA-type sewage treatment system in the '30s that was supposed to be cleaning up the water before it was dumped.

But the bay was getting awful. As San Diego continued to grow, there was a big push in the 1960s to build a sewage treatment system with an outfall at Point Loma. The hero of this project was then-mayor Frank Curran. All of the cities in the metropolitan area banded together in the first cooperative effort to build a local infrastructure that would benefit everyone. The sewage system would stretch from Poway, Santee and Lakeside down to Tijuana. It would be built for growth.

It would have the latest engineering technology and it would cost millions of dollars. But as long as the government would be there to subsidize all these jobs and all these expenses, why not?

So the good citizens of the San Diego metropolitan area passed the bond for the local costs, the feds coughed up the dough and we built it. The sewage was put in big vats, the solids were removed and a biological decay mechanism was added that removed everything else and pumped it into the ocean off Point Loma where there was no thought of any threat to the environment.

At the same time, we agreed that life would be more simple if the Metropolitan Sewer District would be one and the same as the San Diego City Council. Cities in the outlying areas figured they could let San Diego take care of the operational details. Everything was flush.

The sewer system served for many years as a determining factor for growth. Wherever the sewer went in, homes, cars, kids, dogs, cats and schools followed. Until the system filled up. Then more tanks were added, more lines were added and more treatment capacity was added. But the limit of the Point Loma outfall – about 130 million gallons a day – was starting to be a concern.

Then the federal government stepped in with the Clean Water Act, which said that by a certain date in the 1990s all municipal sewage had to have secondary treatment.

Pete Wilson, who was mayor at the time, responded quickly. The Clean Water Act, he reasoned, was passed for the United States because most of the cities are putting sewage in shallow streams, lakes, rivers and other places they shouldn't be putting sewage. San Diego, however, is putting treated sewage water into the Pacific Ocean, which is many miles deep and about 16,000 miles across.

Do the Waive

In 1978, Congress passed waiver legislation into the Clean Water Act that said, if you can prove that you don't need secondary treatment, you don't have to build it. So, San Diego got its waiver. And we renewed the waiver and renewed the waiver again because we didn't have any money to build secondary sewage treatment facilities and we didn't need them.

In February 1987, Mayor Maureen O'Connor and Councilman Mike Gotch spearheaded a movement in the San Diego City Council, which was still also the Metropolitan Sewer District, that set this comfortable situation careening into the unknown. Reject the waiver! they said. We will get federal money from our good friend Senator Alan Cranston and we will comply with secondary treatment.

We care about the environment and we're going to clean up that water before it hits the ocean.

Well, there were some fatal flaws in the plan. They had no idea what it would cost in terms of the environment. They had no idea what it would cost in terms of engineering. They had no idea what it would cost in terms of cost.

Meanwhile, scientists at Scripps Institute of Oceanography, one of the most sophisticated marine biology laboratories in the world, announced that if the water were treated to a secondary level it would NOT improve the ecosystem that has developed in the ocean waters off Point Loma. In fact, the food chain could be deprived of nutrients. If we build it, it will screw things up.

44

Also meanwhile, Alan Cranston, Maureen's good friend, said What? What money? You're on your own. The feds have no money. If we build it, it will cost billions.

Finally, it all ended up in federal court. Judge Rudy Brewster had to decide this entire issue and a preliminary decision came down to side with the scientists and to rule that a secondary treatment plant would not enhance the environment and was not necessary.

Recently the city voted to try and get the waiver back. But the federal government said that there was no such thing as waivers anymore and we will probably be required to comply with the Clean Water Act in the future. We now know that the total project will take ten years to complete and $6 billion in hard costs and double that with interest payments.

Ironically, secondary treatment wasn't even on the city council agenda back in February of 1987. The city manager had suggested a plan that would extend the Point Loma outfall two miles and make the pipeline a "T" to make the dispersal more effective.

If that plan had been adopted, there might have been no blowout in the Spring of 1992, when millions of gallons of semi-treated sewage wound up on our beaches and there were 19 breaks in the pipeline.

How did that happen? We may not ever know. In 1992, the city council called for a study of the break and spent thousands of taxpayer dollars determining what happened. The completed study was banned from release to the general public by the city council. Now, this brings to mind all kinds of imaginative possibilities from a threat to national security by a wayward nuclear missile to a monster from the deep.

45

Most likely, however, the report was just too embarrassing and would make the city council the target of lawsuits. There is talk that the failure analysis notes an air bubble in the pipeline, which might mean somebody was fooling around with a valve somewhere. So there remains a possibility of further ruptures in the system.

The San Diego City Council is still the Metropolitan Sewer District, with no representation from the other cities served by the system. Harriet Stockwell and Lu-Gray Hill, representing El Cajon and La Mesa, formed a coalition in recent years to demand that the district be expanded, redefined and put into the hands of some responsible officials that will pay attention to running it properly. Their demands were insultingly ignored.

Last fall the San Diego City Council added insult to injury and sent out bills doubling the sewer charges, leaving the regions' representatives helpless to guard their constituents against the city's ineptitude.

And it gets worse. Decisions need to be made to get more water from reclamation. Currently, the only water reclamation facility in San Diego sits in Mission Valley near Highways 8 and 805. The city council actually wanted to sell that land to a developer to put up yet another empty high rise office building. Then they were going to turn around and buy another, more expensive lot in Mission Valley and build a new water reclamation facility on it. Luckily the public outcry against such fiscal folly caused them to scrap that plan. But, like many bad ideas, this one could be back.

Political posturing, misplaced environmentalism and fierce territorialism now rule the day. The city council, acting as the Metropolitan

46

Sewer District, is cartwheeling toward a multi-billion dollar disaster and responsible leadership that is not caught up in their game-playing is reaching a new frustration level. If the secrecy and the bad planning and the bully politics don't catch up with them, the consumer outrage and the Clean Water Act requirements will.

When it hits the fan, point it at City Hall.

The Trash Chores

Since day one, San Diego has had all of these wonderful canyons to fill up with trash. One of the original city dumps is located off of Highway 94, and the years of layered trash make a footstool for the precision accuracy of the police pistol practice range. There are a variety of landfill sites around town underneath contrasting modern areas – some are poetic and some are coming back to haunt us.

But trash is a pretty recent phenomenon in San Diego. During World War II, there was no garbage. First of all, there were no goods. But if there were goods, they weren't packaged. Everyone took their cheesecloth bag to the store for flour. Everyone kept their string in a ball. Victory gardens were filled with compost, nails were kept in baby food jars and every available resource was being recycled for the war effort. There was no garbage.

By 1985, however, we were producing more than a ton of throw-away trash for every man, woman and child in San Diego each year. We kept filling up canyons with it until we became aware of the environment. Then, we tried to recycle, but this has continued to falter because it just isn't cost effective. Glass is sand. Paper is wood. Plastic is toxic. It's cheaper to make new than to reprocess the old.

We tried to get creative by gathering all the trash together and burning it to make steam, which could create electricity, which you could sell to pay for the process. But the environment caught us again, because burning all of the complex chemicals that now make up our trash creates such a noxious byproduct that the air gets filled with a cancer-causing cloud. We junked that approach.

San Diego now has a society where there is soon going to be no place to take out the trash. New York now has garbage scows that move up and down the Eastern seaboard and the Caribbean in search of trash dumps. There have been serious proposals to shoot trash into space.

And that's just the benign trash. We've been sensitized to hazardous waste disposal to the point of hysteria. For instance, hospitals and biotech industries have been searching for disposal sites for low-level radioactive waste and have decided on the Ward Valley in the Mojave Desert. Recently there has been some alarm because it is 25 miles away from a canal.

But it's 25 miles of solid rock. And the stuff we are throwing away are gloves and test tubes, not reactor cores. So the public tends to act with tremendous ignorance and distrust on these issues and it has become the plaything of elitist politicians. North County wants to cart its trash into San Marcos and San Marcos will have none of it. Why should Escondido get a shopping center and San Marcos get a landfill?

The City of San Diego's solution is to suggest a charge for trash collection. You've been getting trash collection for free, they announced, now we're going to have to charge. And the constituents said, Gee whiz, I guess they're right.

Until they thought about it for about a minute. When has trash collection ever been free? The city ordinance of 1919 laid out clearly that property taxes collected would pay for trash collected. The new proposed collection fee is a way to make people pay twice. And if the trash collection system has become too expensive for property taxes to pay for, maybe it's time to look again at the system. Maybe recycling just got cheaper.

San Diego is up against a barrier with the sewer pipeline. San Diego is up against a barrier with the landfill. It is the end of an era.

We have come to an end in an era of our history when we believed that all we had to do was work together and we could solve any problems. All we need is a hero with an idea and we can accomplish it. Even if we had the money–if there were $5 billion in the bank for sewer systems–what would we do? We have to plan. We have to pay. Once upon a time in San Diego, there was growth. And growth was good. Need an airport? Sure. More water? Of course. There was a broad-based consensus.

Now nothing can be suggested without a cacophony of dissenting voices. And there is no common will, no political infrastructure, no mechanism allowing the community, in its diversity to gain a consensus and move in the agreed upon direction. And it's not that we don't have enough water, not that we don't have enough sewers, not that we don't have enough canyons to fill with trash. It's that we don't want to grow anymore. The urban sprawl building industry is dead.

But San Diego, of course, will grow. It's just that San Diego must now grow in quality. San Diego can make a conscious decision to be a smaller, large city and to spend public funds on enhancements that will make us an important city.

We have to have the library and make it accessible to every citizen and make it interface with the universities. We need a computer on every telephone. Fiber optics linking every home. We need to realize that the new industries and the new technology that we want to attract will not be done by cheap laborers, but by sophisticated, educated workers.

And if people begin moving out of San Diego instead of moving in (which is a radical reversal of our 120-year history) there will be enough sewer water and landfill capacity for everyone. Here's a radical thought: If we don't build it, it's O.K.

*"I don't like that Hubert H. Humphrey
Metrodome. It's a shame a great guy like
Humphrey had to be named after it."*

– Billy Martin

6

Whatcha Ma Callit

When God created the earth He made every manner of creature in the sea, in the sky and on land. Then He paraded them before Adam and said, "Give them names." The Bible is careful to note that this happened before God made Eve, because He knew that once there were two people in the world, they would never be able to agree on the naming of anything.

As much as we need heroes in San Diego, and as desperately as we are seeking leadership into the next decades, the men and women that we find had better be comfortable with tributes other than have things named after them. It's something we don't do well.

In fact, San Diegans have a great tradition of not being able to come up with good names for things. The result is that we have lots of things named the same, lots of things named after people we don't remember and lots of things with no special name at all.

The region itself was named in controversy. In 1542, Juan Rodriguez Cabrillo discovered our bay and named it Bahia de San Miguel. It was regarded with as a port of no consequence. Sixty years later, Sebastian Vizcaino set sail from Acapulco and made a ten day stop at our bay in his ships, *San Diego*, *Santo Tomas* and *Tres Reyes*. Except for a nudge of history, San Dieguito could have been Tomasito. Since Cabrillo died before he could follow up on his exploration and Vizcaino was on his way to becoming mayor of Acapulco, no one winced when he renamed the bay after his flagship.

San Diego was another name for St. James de Alcala, an obscure Dominican friar in the tiny town of Alcala, Spain. The friar was given sainthood for courage in connection with a Muslim/Christian border dispute, so there is some symmetry to history after all.

We'll Name It After You

Over the years, San Diego landmarks have commemorated those who have contributed to the city in a special way. John D. Spreckels' name lives on in the theater, the organ pavilion and the fountain that he donated to Alonzo Horton for the fledgling Horton Plaza development. Horton himself has been aptly memorialized by the rebuilding of the Horton Grand Hotel and the multi-million dollar shopping center that finally realized his dream of a downtown shopping district.

George Marston, on the other hand, who probably thought that his name would be forever-immortalized by his popular retail stores, chose not to give his name to the land he donated to the city. He named it Presidio Park. Frank Terril Botsford was the single-handed developer of a little beach town to the north, but had the good sense not to use his name to rename La Jolla.

Some names have been used in San Diego to elevate the status of the town. Lindbergh Field was named after the famous aviator, even though his historic flight began in New York and ended in Paris. The main street of downtown, known as 'D' Street in the planning grid, was changed to Broadway to give the town a little class. Early San Diegans hired Kate Sessions to be the cultivator of City Park, which gained sophistication when it was renamed for Balboa.

E.W. Scripps came to San Diego with his first million from a publishing empire and named his land Miramar Ranch. Aside from that, his half-sister Ellen Browning Scripps and his sister, Virginia Scripps joined him in making significant contributions to San Diego in the Scripps name. These include everything from the world-renowned Scripps Institution of Oceanography, Scripps Memorial Hospital, Scripps Clinic and Research Foundation, to the tiny little Scripps Inn in La Jolla.

These days, philanthropists are still commemorated through their donations, i.e., The McDonald Center for substance abuse, the Joan Kroc hospice and homeless center, the Copley Symphony Hall. It's a pretty simple system. You pay, you get your name on it.

Even this can get complicated in San Diego, however. The Gaslamp Quarter Theater began in a tiny venue that became known as the Elizabeth North Theater when the group acquired expanded quarters attached to the Horton Grand Hotel. The new theater was named the Gaslamp Quarter Theater, until a man named Deanne gave a donation that caused it to be named the Deanne Theater. That relationship soured and Deanne had his name removed from the theater and a restraining order placed against his identification with the theater in any way. It is now called the Hahn Cosmopolitan Theater. Guess who paid the bill.

When it comes to civic projects, where everybody pays, that's when things can get really interesting in San Diego. The stadium in Mission Valley was built to put the name of San Diego on lips across the nation. The Copley newspapers, however, had a different agenda and forced a vote that gave that tribute to its late sports columnist, Jack Murphy.

Perhaps even more significant is the lack of name identification with so many of our projects. No one has gotten their name on the Sports Arena, the Civic Auditorium, or, as yet, the Convention Center.

Change It to What?

Not that they haven't tried. The very worst example of San Diego's naming efforts was the proposal to rename Market Street to Martin Luther King Blvd. This was the brainstorm of a City Council committee, which proposed it even though all of the merchants on Market Street were resisting the change and all of the merchants on Imperial Avenue, one block away, *did* want the name. They were ignored, however, and the city council rubber stamped the committee's proposal.

Immediately there followed a grass-roots petition drive to force a public vote. The new street signs were made and installed. The public said no.

To save face, the city council then went to the Port District and tried to get them to give the name to the Convention Center. That put the Port District in the embarrassing position of saying, No, thank you, but we have a name and it's the San Diego Convention Center. Afterward, there was some talk at the Port District of creating an Avenue of Champions with Dr. King as the first honoree, but this did not get the city off the hook.

Eventually, the City Council negotiated that a downtown trolley strip would be named Martin Luther King Park, even though there already is a Martin Luther King Park in San Diego. And they took part of a highway and called it Martin Luther King Highway. That started a trend. North County jumped on the highway bandwagon and created Ted Williams highway out of North City Parkway, which had always been a confusing name anyway. There is no North City.

Richard Silberman was honored by having his name placed on a highway bridge and the citizens of San Diego thought highly enough of the honor to revoke it when Silberman was convicted of money laundering. There was a movement to create a Cara Knott Road after the young girl who was raped and murdered by a California Highway Patrol officer, but it was decided that Mercy Road could keep it's name and still invoke a memorial to Knott.

All in all, we just aren't that adept at names and maybe we should give up trying. The Intercontinental Hotel is now the Marriott; the Omni is now the Doubletree; the Doubletree is now the Hilton. If we wait long enough, the name will change.

If we are truly seeking to be a world-class city, why not let all of San Diego become, in effect, a Hall of Champions, where projects, buildings and roadways commemorate learning, discovery, training, and human achievement throughout the globe. We may learn something about the rest of the world and we may even agree. Call me crazy.

*"Why can't we have those curves and arches
that express feeling in design? What is wrong
with them? Why has everything got to be verti-
cal, straight, unbending, only at right angles –
and functional?"*

– Prince of Wales

7

I Know It When I See It

Back in the last decades of the last century, when Alonzo Horton was scrambling to make the City of San Diego into "Old Town" and to make his New Town into the City of San Diego, there wasn't much time to think about art. We weren't too worried about leadership in terms of architecture. The new downtown was being built with pre-fabricated store-fronts and the streets were made of clay.

By the end of the 1880s, however, the land boom had produced a small community of people with wealth that had arrived from other places. They wanted San Diego to look better, so a veneer of civilization was applied. The buildings began to be more substantial. John D. Spreckels built his theater with flair. The U.S. Grant Hotel added grandeur to the town. The name of "D" street was changed to Broadway. In one of the first private donations of public art, Spreckels donated a fountain, designed by Irving Gill, to Horton Plaza. The link between art and the economy was discovered. If it looks good, they will come.

It Pays To Be Pretty

In the '30s the link between art and economy was discovered by the government. At that time, the WPA began to support public art as a means of uplifting the human spirit. Art became viewed as it had always been viewed by the great art patrons of Europe – as propaganda. The WPA-built San Diego County Administration Building was graced with a sculpture, Guardian of the Water, designed by Donal Hord, to express the harmony of a beneficent government conquering nature to serve mankind. The same sculptor created the Aztec Chief on Montezuma Mesa at SDSU to artfully ennoble the American natives who had been mercilessly driven off and made destitute by the U.S. government only decades earlier. Art as propaganda.

Recently, the strapped city budget funded an exhibition in Casa de la Raza in Balboa Park which displayed Fidel Castro's anti-American propaganda videos. The public was outraged. Propaganda as art.

Evidence of the interdependency of art and government can be seen throughout San Diego. The Civic Auditorium was built as a part of the city's administration complex in order to lure opera, symphony and ballet companies from Los Angeles and San Francisco to perform here. This infusion of culture to build up the city had been going on since Lillie Langtry performed in 1888 to give validity to the boom-town status of Horton's Addition.

In the '60s, San Diego started COMBO - the Combined Arts Organization - to serve as a clearing house for grant funding. The brilliant idea of the Tourist Occupancy Tax (TOT) had been approved by voters with the belief that the hotels should subsidize the activities that were need to bring the Smiths and Joneses from their homes in the Midwest to the fancy hotels in San Diego. From that time on, anything that happened in terms of art in San Diego was marked by a partnership of private and public funding.

Which made it just that much harder to define. Our northern neighbors in Laguna Beach have made it a source of civic pride to appreciate art, understand art, allow art to expand and be a part of the city's culture. The Laguna Art Festival, when it became politicized and stodgy, made way for the Sawdust Festival, that provided for alternative expressions of creativity. This has been growing and expanding for over 20 years. Meanwhile, in La Jolla, the galleries are still selling cowboys on horseback. On of the most popular exhibits ever displayed at the San Diego Museum of Art honored the illustrations of Dr. Seuss. Great, but is that art?

And, who says so? Public funding begets public controversy.

Recently the Museum of Contemporary Art, San Diego, formerly the San Diego Museum of Contemporary Art, formerly the La Jolla Museum of Contemporary Art, took hits for its display of parts of the private collection of Bill Koch, winner of the America's Cup. Here was a wealthy, albeit temporary resident of San Diego who had collected various works of arts at his various homes throughout the world. The idea of putting them together in one big room and calling it an exhibit offended even the blunted sensibilities of the average citizen, let alone the regular museum supporters.

Because, although we may not always know how to define, describe or create art, we sure do know what isn't art. A few years ago, the Port District agreed that San Diego should have some public art to enhance the bay. It should be spectacular. It should be a statement about San Diego. So an international search was made to find an artist who could make a statement about San Diego and the commission was given to Vito Acconci.

The problem was, the statement that the Acconci wanted to make about San Diego was to place a plane wreckage and concrete palm trees near Lindbergh Field, often considered the world's most dangerous landing strip. No way, said San Diego. That ain't art. So we caused an international furor and were labeled as boorish and provincial.

Meanwhile, the owner of Classic Reprographics, under the flight path on Fourth Avenue, got his own plane, painted it hot pink, jammed it down on the roof of his building and everybody saw it and everybody loved it.

Horton Plaza is still a very visible focal point of art, and may be the most definitive San Diego art of all, capturing our enthusiasm of the moment and our identity-of-the-week mentality in brick, mortar, stucco and wood. Horton Plaza incorporates every architectural reference from the Egyptian obelisk of the Lyceum to the mission tower of Nordstrom to the Jessop's clock. But it is all well done, fun to explore and doesn't take itself too seriously. On the other hand, the Omni San Diego Hotel tried to play catch-up with its adjacent neighbor and put its own sculpture out there. The huge plastic blue glob looks like an aquarium toy gone mad. That ain't art.

At the same time Horton Plaza was thrusting new ideas at us, the Gaslamp Quarter Council hired Art Skolnik at a very inflated salary to fly down every week from Seattle to tell us what historic restoration should look like. That was a lot easier to handle. When in doubt, restore. So we restored the U.S. Grant Hotel at an enormous expense and helped break the bank. We restored the Fox Theater into the glorified Symphony Hall and had to be bailed out of debt by Helen Copley. There is a board of directors that keeps revolving around the idea of restoring the Balboa Theater, but it has never been able to get any kind of support for the project. Restoration is not the only answer.

But the one thing that Art Skolnik, along with determined efforts by Judy Lenthall and Gloria Poore, did for San Diego before he high-tailed it away was to push for and win the passage of a Loft Ordinance so that the beginnings of an art culture, an art community, could be established. It created at least the structure for art to be defined by us. For an indigenous art to be born. Each year ArtWalk has celebrated this creativity with moderate funding and diminishing success.

Because, no matter how much cappuccino you can buy, how many interesting clothes you can find, how much provocative furniture you can see, or how many fascinating crafts are displayed, the Loft district has yet to produce any spectacular art or genius artists from within its free-form borders. In time, it may.

But San Diego continues to define its look through the contest mentality. If a group of people will tell us how we can look, we'll decide which one we like best. We are caught up in design by committee which is, to quote one local artist, how God made the bird of paradise. A little of that and one of these. The crisis of San Diego leadership in terms of public art, architecture and city planning is beginning to create a hodge-podge of styles that makes Horton Plaza look homogeneous.

In 1988, a delightful slide show was developed by the San Diego Planning Department to show the glaring disparity in downtown lighting fixtures. It included converted gaslamps, great winged modern lamps, sleek post-war designs, and more. Often two or three styles can be found in the same block, all of them painted different colors. The visual evidence, laid out as a whole, prompted action and the city took a bold stand. All street lights would be painted blue. Not monumental, maybe, but a start. Now they can work on getting rid of the gruesome yellow bulbs.

San Diego, has been on a course of building and growth. During the '80s, plans were developed that would heighten the skyline increase density and service an expanded population. It's time to take a second look. One hundred years after the first land boom bust, when ten thousand residents left town within a month, we have to begin anticipating what San Diego can look like on a smaller-than-Los Angeles scale. There are still a number of projects to be completed that will define the visual character of downtown – the Navy's public/private embarcadero project, the proposed library, the possibility of a Sports Arena, the expansion of the Convention Center.

Commercial growth may be stunted, but these civic projects should happen. The design of these projects, the public art linking them together, as well as the details such as walkways, public seating, landscaping and scale, are waiting for a champion.

Someone must sit down with CCDC, the CCA Design Committee, Mike Stepner, Ernest Hahn, Ron Hahn, Doug Manchester, the Port District, Seaport Village and the Convention and Visitor's Bureau, and say, This is what we are, this is what we should be, these are the limits of our funds and the horizons of our vision. Now, go build.

"When politicians and civil servants hear the word 'culture' they feel for their blue pencil."

– Lord Esher

8

The Play's the Thing

Act One

The theater has always been a place to see and be seen in San Diego. From the very beginning when Horton Hall, located at 6th and F streets, opened its doors in 1882, San Diego has always found entertainment in the live arts to be the genteel type of nightlife that lent dignity to the dusty streets, the false storefronts and the bawdy back alleys that made up much of downtown. In 1888, the famous Lillie Langtry of New Jersey arrived in town in her private rail car and sang to a sold-out crowd of stunned San Diegans. We have been in awe over outside entertainment ever since.

In 1935, the Old Globe Theater was built as a part of the California Pacific International Exposition. The Shakespearean venue reinforced the idea that the best play was one that had already been seen before and that we could count on outsiders to identify good theater for us. It's the same mentality that has kept the San Diego Civic Light Opera alive through years of name changes and venue switches. But those good old favorites have always found a comfortable audience in San Diego and have finally allowed the Starlight to come inside for the winter in the restored Spreckel's Theater, still standing proudly on Broadway.

The La Jolla Playhouse entered the picture in the '40s as stars from Hollywood discovered the shoreline resort and the beauties of sand, sea and La Valencia. Film stars appreciated the challenge of "real'" acting, the honored status that La Jolla society gave them and the chance to get away from the politics of the Hollywood star system.

Act Two

By the early 1980's San Diego was poised to have an explosion in theater participation. The Gaslamp Quarter Theater, led by the creative gumption of Kit Goldman, was bursting its seams. The Lamb's Players were producing consistent winners in their own niche; the La Jolla Playhouse had a new theater venue in the works and the Old Globe was re-establishing itself after its second devastating fire. In addition, the creative team of Sam Woodhouse and Doug Jacobs had long been making the San Diego Repertory Theater a contender for theater-lovers, with a growing creativity and a sharpening professionalism. Groups like the Bowery Theater were springing up and the Sushi Gallery, with its wild performance art, was gaining in stature. Everybody was finding an audience.

And everybody was going. During the '80s all subscriptions in town were growing. As the yuppies scurried around getting dates, theater-going became chic. As corporations looked for visible means of showing support for the community, theater grants made good business sense. As a means of supporting tourist interest and convention trade, civic dollars were sent to the stage. Newer, bigger and better stages were built. We built them. They came. The expansion was like a rocket and the choices for theater-lovers were thrilling. All of this momentum started to pay off for San Diego theater. The San Diego Repertory Theater's "Holy Ghosts" traveled to New York's Joyce Theater for the American Theater Exchange. The La Jolla Playhouse took "Big River" to New York and won a Tony.

New challenges were presented to audiences in plays like Peter

Sellars' "Visions of Simone Machard" and "Ajax," Stephen Metcalfe's "Emily." Even the Starlight made a reach by presenting "Evita" and "Jesus Christ, Superstar."

"Slingshot," presented by the REP in connection with the Russian arts festival was, perhaps, the ultimate challenge. Written by a Russian playwright, Nikilai Colyada, and translated a scant few weeks before opening, the powerful and tragic ravings of a isolated and perverted amputee, mixed with radiant spiritual fantasies that offered little hope was a raw look at Soviet Russia in, what we now know to be, the last stages of its death throes.

San Diegans didn't want to touch it with a ten-foot pole. That play, as well as that year, ushered in another next change.

Speaking with Kirsten Brandt at the REP, Francine, who was writing reviews at the time, spoke up. "Look at the change in the culture," she said, "We are entering the years of nostalgia. The boomers are growing up remembering the good old days. You need to tap into to that, put out a remake of 'Hair.' "

A few weeks later Kirsten called back. "You'll love this, Francine. We're doing "The Rocky Horror Show."

So, ninety-nine years after San Diegans went to the theater to be seen as refined and dignified, we raised eyebrows at Horton Plaza wearing wild finery to opening night of every baby boomer's bad boy fantasy production. We called it, "Cross-Dress for Success."

The nostalgia-on-stage era has been profitable for San Diego theaters, with "Suds," "Beehive," "Forever Plaid," and others entertaining huge audiences. Now their remake of the rock musical "Tommy" engineered by Des McAnuff, is being launched on a national scale, which will, again, establish San Diego as a place that is finally able to tell other cities what plays to see.

Today, San Diego theater-goers are being recognized as some of the most sophisticated and diverse of all regional theaters in the country. The outsiders, who tell us what a good play is, are now us.

Act Three

It is the '90s and San Diego is in a recession. The great corporate funding is down to a trickle. Banks have closed and bank executives are unemployed instead of major donors. Businesses have stopped giving their top people season tickets and are giving them boxes of their names spelled in chocolate. It's a new era.

What will happen to the momentum? What will happen to the words and the sets and the music? Will the curtain be drawn, the lights go off and the stage, stark and bare, be silent?

Not necessarily. But new audiences have to be cultivated and we need to find more stage room. The San Diego Repertory Theater was awarded the Lila Wallace-Reader's Digest Resident Theater Initiative grant because they have aggressively sought audiences from ethnic communities. Their offerings for 1992-93 include plays from the African-American, Asian, Hispanic and Jewish cultures, with last two seasons including over 50% of their artists being artists of color. The REP continues to provide school children with theater experiences and fights to keep theater-going a priority for all San Diegans.

Alternative theater groups, the Diversionary Theater, Labrys, Sledgehammer Theater, Blackfriars Theater and the Fritz are also a very important part of an active theater culture. These experiments and risk-taking productions are going to keep us thinking and growing.

So is our participation.

The Christian Youth Theater, which provides acting and theatrical training for kids, has grown from a weekly class in a La Mesa church to a county-wide industry, with classes offered throughout San Diego and several performances staged each year. The adult division, Christian Community Theater, presents plays every summer. The San Diego Junior Theater has been successful for years. This over-abundance of activity should be telling the theatrical community something.

San Diegans want to participate. We want to act, sing, direct and perform. Have you been to a karaoke bar, open mike night at a coffeehouse or opera night at the Better Worlde Galleria? San Diegans are out there. The way we feel about sports, is the way we feel about performance. Let us get up on stage, write our own plays, read our poetry, sing our songs and have our fifteen minutes of fame.

If theater is going to continue to thrive in San Diego, the major theater groups need to keep cultivating this drive to perform and this passion for live art. Interaction with the stage, actors and directors should not be limited to discussions and tours. How about a workshop? A rehearsal? An open audition?

Jeff Shohet, president of the REP board, joked that he wanted to be cast in a REP play and the staff joked back that he could be the next Scrooge in "A Christmas Carol."

But was he kidding?

Craig Noel of the Old Globe admits that his subscription solicitations are limited to 5% of the population. Yet the discount ArtsTix had a blowout sale recently that drew a line of people blocks long. People want to come. They want to be involved.

The San Diego theater community will continue to grow as audiences are redefined, barriers are crossed and stories expanded. The REP is leading the way toward the next generation of theater-goers and is a model of ethnic expansion. The La Jolla Playhouse's Des McAnuff is making inroads with Los Angeles and New York producers who are recognizing San Diegans as a sophisticated and provocative audience.

In addition, a new generation of performance is opening up, as recent UCSD graduates are exploring some new multi-level performance options and non-linear works are becoming more acceptable. We have become the cutting edge. But it will take commitment from the community, businesses and government to keep us there.

But we need more space. Right now San Diego theater can put on a show with the best of them. We have the creativity, the talent, the actors and actresses, the production talent, the musical talent, the sophistication for top-notch theater. But, once we have a hit, there is no place to put it. "Tommy" could be running in San Diego to full houses for a good year if there were a place for it to roost. The Playhouse could be in the black forever. "Forever Plaid" is making its third reprisal at the Old Globe. If there were a stage to put it on, money would be pouring in. We have discovered how to get the plays to the point of perfection, now we have to take the next step and find a way to keep them playing long enough to make money.

If we are to become the new San Diego, the San Diego where people are exposed to new thought, new technology, new ways of living, new ways of relating to other countries – then the stretch that all theater provides, light entertainment, classics, proven Broadway spectacles and ethnic and provocative theater is very important to our future. When all of the rest of our civic identities have come and gone, the business trends have been played out, the politics shifted sides, the tourist attractions seen and forgotten – it may very well be the arts that ultimately define San Diego to the rest of the world.

The largest theatrical institutions in San Diego have had stable artistic leadership in place for over ten years now. These heroes have provided real roots in our cultural landscape. And if we can keep these roots nurtured, watered and protected, perhaps our theaters will not be like tumbleweeds, blowing away, but like trees, offering shade to all of us.

"If begging should unfortunately be thy lot,
knock at the large gates only."

– Arabian proverb

9

Dancing For Diseases

San Diegans are a generous lot. When the symphony was threatened with bankruptcy several years ago, musicians played on street corners and funds came in from elders on Social Security, children's allowances and from folks who said, "I don't really like classical music, but I think we should have a symphony."

But there is an entire segment of our culture that has shown leadership again and again in improving the quality of life in San Diego. These donors have been heroic in rescuing not only our institutions, but in easing the plight of those who are helpless and suffering. They make their homes in La Jolla.

La Jolla is a state of mind. Nestled underneath the Torrey Pines cliffs, La Jolla stretches to include the sophistication of Black's Beach where gay patrons maintain a dignified nudity, to the frolicking squeals of the Children's Pool. La Jolla preserves the rock-solid American values of clean, good living, exercise, salads for lunch, late gourmet dinners, picnics on the beach, father/son surfing, debutante balls and Important people doing Important things. And the thing that makes them Important is money.

From the earliest days of the La Jolla Beach and Tennis Club, where membership is passed on through the generations, to the more recent rosters of the La Jolla Country Club; between the Bishop's School and La Jolla Country Day School; from getting your favorite table at the Whaling Bar to having your special wine at George's, exclusivity has been part of the La Jolla culture. It's that elusive factor that makes for a self-celebrated community. In fact, it's the exact opposite of San Diego's self-esteem crisis. If it's La Jollan, it has to be special. That is why, although officially part of the City of San Diego, La Jolla has its own zip code and post office. It has its own telephone directory. It has its own rules.

But the rules are simple. Yes, you may have money, but you also have a responsibility to give it away. And you can't just give it away, you have to use it to raise more. So, above the demure, sometimes pampered, always stylish, size eight figures that shop Jonathan's and Adelaide's are some of the most savvy, professional and cost-conscious fund-raisers in Southern California. These women are executives. Their committees are their employees. Their charities are their product.

Dorene Whitney took on the gala opening of Symphony Hall in 1986 like a business. For more than a year before the event, she wheeled and dealed to get underwriting, to get pre-payments deposited at the highest of interest rates, to find subsidies and to make the event a success. In one evening, the symphony raised several hundreds thousand dollars. When she chaired the opening gala for the San Diego Opera the next year, she raised another incredible amount of money, including $5,000 in raffle tickets sold during the half-hour before breakfast.

Whitney's latest efforts have taken her to Washington, D.C., where she chaired the effort for the restoration of the First Lady's gowns on display at the Smithsonian Institution. From her apartment at the Watergate complex, Whitney has been able to walk in power corridors that make La Jolla's complexities seem mild. Yet sitting at the Whaling Bar one day she watched a group of women gossiping at the next booth and told Francine, "It's impossible to have a real friend in this town."

Around the same years, Nancy Hester and Mac Canty started the La Jolla Off the Wall party on Wall Street. Nancy's charitable events were marked by fun – a dog fashion show and a black-tie car wash. Young women have introduced new ways to raise funds and newer groups, like the Child Abuse Prevention Foundation, have called for their volunteers to do hands-on advocacy as well as fund-raising.

The contributions to San Diego that have been made by these volunteers runs into the millions, and the thanks afforded them is often little more than a photo in the *La Jolla Light* or a name in *San Diego Magazine*. As a result, these two chronicles of society activity are a large part of the scheme that perpetuates the charitable giving and keeps those volunteers coming back for more. David Nelson of the *L.A. Times*, Jeanne Eigner and the venerable Burl Stiff of the *San Diego Union/Tribune* have the power to celebrate these contributions or to dismiss them, as any organization planning a gala is sure to discover. As Janet Gallison, the former *La Jolla Light* society columnist once remarked, "No one has a party anymore just for fun. It always has to be for a cause."

Yuppie Giving

But in the heady, yuppie growth spurt of the '80s, a new facet of charitable contributions was tapped in San Diego. The singles.

Suddenly venerable La Jolla philanthropists were ousted from society columns by young, cute singles who were discovering their civic responsibilities to San Diego and fulfilling them by planning fund-raising events on a mass scale.

Don McVey, a young attorney, started it all. He came to San Diego, saw that most cultural events involved older people who were married and who had lots of money, and decided to change all of that. McVey created the San Diego League to bring bright young singles together for charitable purposes. The yuppie charities were born. He soon had established a mailing list of single professionals with money, time, and a driving need to meet other singles in an appropriate set-ting. How could it miss? They started with some small gatherings, then took the plunge and sponsored the first New Year's Eve gala at the brand new Horton Plaza. Thousands came. Singles events were born.

And they kept coming. Suddenly, singles clubs were formed for theater-going, dining out and doing taxes. Singles went to sock hops, costume parties, the races, wine-tasting events, faux skiing parties and black-tie casino nights. As one single gentleman said, "Why pay $50 for a date with one woman when I can spend that at a singles event and meet one hundred?" And it all went to charity.

Or did it? Because, before too long, some of these group leaders figured out how to cash in. In one case, the director of the single's group had his girlfriend on the payroll and was getting free hotel rooms, tax deductible computers, cellular phones and other perks because of his charitable involvement.

By the end of the '80s, the trend had peaked. Visa cards were maxed. Lots of people who started the decade single had found mates and started families. Discretionary dollars dried up and the creative and dynamic leadership that started these groups got diffused. The singles that worked so hard to put on these events have started to mainstream through the charitable boards, auxiliaries and clubs that were more traditional. Don McVey got married.

And La Jolla changed. The overdevelopment of the little beach town has driven many residents into Del Mar and Rancho Santa Fe. There are foreigners at La Valencia, strangers at Harry's for breakfast. It's not the same.

The era of generous philanthropy may be ending. How many more times can the Symphony say to the community, we have used up our cash reserves? Particularly after announcing that Symphony Towers would ensure that they would never be short of money again.

How many times can you race through Neiman-Marcus looking for clues and prizes? How many more times can you dance around the La Jolla Marriott? Is the party over?

There are other ways. Founded by Dr. Bob Deane and a small group of friends at Lubach's Bar, a group of business people – men and women – have been raising money under the name, "Nice Guys." The Nice Guy of the Year banquet and a Spring auction are two events which have allowed this fun-loving group to escape the formality of galas and balls. It's sort of Blue Collar Meets A Thousand Points of Light when these Nice Guys apply their proceeds not to other organizations but directly to needy people with no other hope. This direct-giving, no overhead approach has attracted more than $1 million and a legion of grateful recipients.

Not So Fast

Today, people who are in the position to give large sums of money to a cause want more for their contribution than a snapshot in the media or a gold plaque. People are asking questions and they want answers. What is the overhead of the organization? What are their politics? How will that organization use the money and what, exactly, will be the result? The whole cause-marketing and "giving back" volunteerism scheme of the last decade is passe. They have given back enough and its time for the city and county to add their share to build up business, ease restrictions and allow entrepreneurs to thrive.

There will always be traditions of giving among those with money to give. The Charity Ball, the oldest gala in San Diego, will hold court at the Hotel del Coronado as grandsons and grandmothers continue the family tradition of sharing a waltz there. The Jewel Ball, now internationally famous, will continue to draw a summer society crowd from Texas, Arizona and beyond who come to town for the racing season. New Year's Eve, now celebrated at the Convention Center, will always be a night for fun and wildness. But will we dance for lung disease or eat chocolate for cancer? For these charities to ride out the recession, they may need to downscale their efforts, stop trying to entertain the patrons and simply ask for the money. Then maybe people will start having parties again. Just for fun.

"Man is born to believe. And if no Church comes forward...to guide him, he will find altars and idols in his own heart and his own imagination."

– Benjamin Disraeli

10

Keeping the Faith

San Diego was discovered by Europeans who roamed the seas for new worlds in search of land, riches and converts. Father Junipero Serra held on to the small San Diego mission years later with determination and some legendary, if not miraculous help.

In fact, the first miracle recorded in San Diego occurred when the good father insisted that a dubious worker apply a donkey poultice to the father's torn, infected feet. The animal remedy cured Padre Serra and a miracle was declared. Some would say that certain religious notions in San Diego still come borrowed from an ass. The need for religious leadership here has made San Diego a crosscurrents, if not a riptide, of spiritual thought.

But in the early days, Catholics were the first San Diegans and they remain, despite a somewhat Midwestern Methodist atmosphere, the largest religious population of the county.

Then came the Baptists. After the Civil War, Americans from the South flooded into San Diego to get away from the sweeping reforms of that region and start anew in a town without prejudice. With these believers came an evangelistic fervor that has made its impact on religious behavior in San Diego to this day. The Catholics understood the Baptists. They didn't like them, but they understood them.

But the Catholics and the Baptists alike were horrified by the Mormons. Mormons practiced their religion in San Diego with quiet determination to break from Utah, but cling to their beliefs. There is a shrine in Old Town today that commemorates the contribution that Mormon Battalion made to the American troops in the war of 1848. The Mormon church supported the war effort with volunteerism and money, which served to help officials look the other way at the illegal practice of bigamy, which was thriving here at the time.

New Age Explosion

Even though these three religious traditions have dominated San Diego, there has always been an attraction in San Diego to more off-beat beliefs. In fact, every wacko religious system on earth has had a presence in San Diego and has received a following of some sort, for some time. We have become the most religiously diverse community in the United States, mixing old traditions with new age twists, funda-mentalists with Taoists, charismatics with ascetics.

Part of the reason for this rests in the fact that no matter how tra-ditional a religious background a person may have, San Diego is bound to put its own stamp on it. Father Serra was sent to the farthest, most insignificant outpost of the Church when he was sent to San Diego. His theology was shaped by drought, encounters with Native Americans, the desire to build a mission and the need for trade. Ever since then, people coming here have brought their traditions and have tweaked them to fit the San Diego priorities of fierce individualism, worship of leisure and fun and tolerance of other religions. Our doc-trines reflects our cultural attitude.

By guaranteeing religious freedom, our forefathers guaranteed that someone would always be able to come along and stir up religious thought and zeal. Far from a lack of religious practice, San Diegans can find an abundance of churches in every neighborhood filled each week. Mini-malls have been filled with Sunday Schools. Civic halls are filled with new age disciples. Yet, you rarely hear about it.

Because inherent to San Diego's lifestyle is a willingness to let people "do their own thing." The last shred of religious intolerance that made La Jolla an exclusively non-Jewish community was kicked off the Torrey Pines cliffs when UCSD was established a little more than 25 years ago. Since then, San Diegans have figured out that they can either be offended by everyone or offended by no one. Most of us choose the latter.

Until last year, when one man, Howard Kreisler, declared that he was offended by the memorial crosses placed on Mt. Soledad and Mt. Helix. He sued the City and the County and a federal judge finally agreed with him and demanded the removal of the crosses. Obviously, this judge knew nothing about San Diego religion.

We are all offended by each other's religions; it's the nature of San Diego. And the idea that one judge can make a ruling on one part of this vast, complicated spiritual dance is absurd. What if they were trying this in Europe? If someone in a European country tried to remove all religious references, there would be no art, no buildings, no street names, no monuments. It's a denial of their whole history.

It's a denial of our whole history, too. One of the great moments of American history was the fundamentalist revival at the turn of the century. It was just after the Spanish/American war and the United States had returning veterans who were hooked on cocaine, breaking up their families and turning to urban crime. It was the Vietnam of 1898. In 1899 the U.S. Navy built its first installations on our shores and droves of young men came to San Diego. The church people wanted these young men in church and the Mexicans wanted them in Tijuana. In effect, the church people created Tijuana. But they cleaned up San Diego.

At the same time this was happening, Katherine Tingsley founded the Universal Theosophical Society brought her mixture of Russian spiritualism and Indian philosophy to Point Loma. She founded the School for the Revival of Lost Mysteries of Antiquity and by the end of the century had homeless Cuban children shipped to San Diego as a relief project.

This blending of religion and social action is deeply rooted in San Diego history. It was the conviction that fostered the Christian Women's Temperance Movement to combat alcoholism and was the inspiration that caused hundreds of Christian women to descend upon the infamous Stingaree District and put prostitutes on the train out of town.

During World War II San Diego religious forces had to work their way around the defense industry, which again took priority over every other concern. After Pearl Harbor, there were condom machines installed all over San Diego – at the Seven Seas Locker, the Hollywood Theater or the Tower Theater. Any arcade on lower Broadway furnished the prophylactics at the urging of the Department of Defense. Right or wrong, said Defense, we want healthy boys going to die in the Pacific.

On the other hand, imminent death had a way of bringing religion to the foreground. San Diego became a strong foothold for the

Navigators and other Christian groups that focused on saving th
souls of Navy boys away from home. For as many sailors who cam
here to lose their virginity were those who came here and found faith.

By the 1950s, San Diego was again dealing with post-war soci;
conditions that were extreme. In 1956, a tent was erected on the are
near Morena Blvd. and a huge revival meeting was held. Hundreds (
San Diegans confessed their sins and confirmed their salvatio
through belief in Christ. Churches grew, Sunday Schools were packe
with little Baby Boomers and our civic policies again reflected stron
accompanying values of family life, crime control, substance abus
protection and limits on adult pleasures.

During the '60s and '70s, when God died in America and th
Beatles were more popular than Christ, religion still thrived in Sa
Diego. By the end of that era, the evangelical Christians were bent o
putting a Christian in the White House and the beginning seeds of
revival of Chrisan fundamentalist politics were established.

Civic Religion

These seeds, by 1992, have grown into a thorny bracket that is threa
ening to choke all the impulses of spiritual renewal from our battere
souls. It has confused the role of religion. Is it a lifestyle or a belief sy;
tem? Should it guide our public mores, or just our private morality?
is a civil right, or is it not? These political Christians are not evange
cal in the sense of preaching the gospel and converting people t
belief in Jesus Christ. Today, these Christians are interested in forcin

ll people to live by their Christian values or be punished. In a society where individual liberty has always been the cornerstone of success, not government, the fundamentalists want to use government to force people to behave.

It doesn't work. It didn't work for the socialists, it didn't work for FDR, it didn't work for LBJ and it certainly will not work for the religionists in San Diego.

If you have the religious conviction that abortion is wrong, for instance, you have every right to take a stand. You have every right to preach that and every right to use whatever legal means are available to convince people of that. But you have no right to force people to act on your own belief. The absolute core doctrine of the Catholic Church and all Christianity is free will. Every day you make choices that are between you and God.

What we *are* sorely lacking in San Diego is religious unity regarding our core values. How do we draft a consensus of religious groups who will attack the real evils in our society – drug trafficking, wife battering, child abandonment, job discrimination, hunger? How can we get religious unity enough to rally around the real problems in the community that demand long-term solutions such as opportunities for education and employment?

We are very good at choosing single-issue concerns. True to our heritage in San Diego, we follow the lead of a strong individual to solve our problems, even though religious leaders are few and far between. Father Joe Carroll is a model of the single hero who can rally ecumenical religious and non-religious support for a single concern.

Father Joe Carroll was a quiet priest who, for most of his career, led a quiet ministry. He was blissfully second in command, in a parish somewhere in the Imperial Valley, when he began to long for a greater impact. His Bishop said, I'll give you a challenge. Go take over the St. Vincent de Paul ministry in urban San Diego. The store is losing money, the care for the homeless is a hopeless battle. Go see what you can do.

Maybe it was the times, maybe it was his age, maybe it was luck and maybe it was divine, but he was the right man for the right job at the right time in the right place. Father Joe rose to the occasion and became a meteor. He became a hustler, an entrepreneur, a leader, a molder and he never took "no" for an answer. Father Joe Carroll changed the whole outlook that people had on the homeless by building the only center in the United States ever built specifically to serve the needs of homeless men, women and children.

So through religious leadership, an impact is being made on a problem – homelessness – that has been shuffled between the city, the county, law enforcement, civic groups and business organizations, all throwing up their hands and turning away.

But even with the model of Father Joe creating coalitions of religious support to attack social ills, that is still not the true role of religious life in San Diego. Because the root cause of all our ills is the lack of values in individuals. People have lost their rudder and there is no longer any connection between what we call civilization and the behavior of people.

Normal Is Getting Worse

Sixteen-year-olds are shooting each other, children are stealing and women are being beaten. It's not just getting more attention. It's happening more often, in more places, to more of our neighbors. It's getting worse. Why? Individuals will no longer take responsibility for themselves. It used to be that societal expectations put people in a holding pattern. You didn't beat your wife because the neighbors would hear and you would be embarrassed by it and they would tell your brother-in-law who lived down the street and your boss might find out and fire you.

These connections created a safety net that held your extreme impulses in check. That is no longer true in San Diego. Now, if you beat your wife, the neighbors will avoid you, your brother-in-law lives in Chicago and your boss could care less.

There must be a revival of the basic, core values that have been held in common by society for centuries. It will take a determined, private leadership to do it, not government action. We can spend money on law enforcement, welfare, jails and judges and it will be very expensive. Or you can save souls for free.

And if the religious people in San Diego don't provide the leadership, it may very likely come from the corporate sector. Just as corporations in the '90s are shoving aside educational requirements and spending $30 billion on reading, writing and other skills to recreate and rebuild the work force; corporations may take the lead in re-establishing incentives for honesty and morality in our hearts.

David Thomas is the owner of Wendy's, a fast-food chain named after his daughter. Many know of his successful operation, which has 65,000 employees. What people don't know is that he was orphaned at birth and was raised by three separate sets of step-parents. This scenario usually spells failure, but Thomas' determination allowed him to overcome these disadvantages. He went on to have a very precious family of his own, including the famous Wendy.

Recently Thomas made public the facts of his life and announced that Wendy is about to give birth to twins. This has prompted him to come up with a new policy. His company will give a cash subsidy to any employee of his who adopts a child. All children deserve a home, reasoned Thomas, and I'm going to back up that conviction with dollars. He announced that he would give $4,500 cash to adoptive parents employed by him and he called on every company in America to consider doing the same. If we don't do this, he said, we will no longer have customers, we'll have looters.

Now this is a relatively small pebble in the pond of society, but it has created a ripple. And if other pebbles follow, it can created a tidal wave of support for a change in values.

The need of this change is resonating throughout San Diego. We who, for so many years, personified freedom from tradition, the place to get away from restrictions and "do your own thing," are now saying "Whoa!" to the whole situational ethics, lack of expectations, removal of morality mess. We are searching for a new social contract, new covenant, new compact. We feel the need to save our souls. And it won't come from right-wing legislation and it won't come from humanistic social action and it won't come from corporate morality. It will come from strong religious leadership, preaching with conviction, leading by example and guiding people through spiritual conversion to a life of wholeness and peace.

"To be able to fill leisure intelligently is the last product of civilization."

– Bertrand Russell

11

All Contractors Are Surfers

Leisure is a primal force in San Diego. Let's admit it. If we really were totally ambitious, Type-A, driven folks, we would be in L.A. working 15 hours a day and pulling in mega-bucks. But those of us who have chosen not to be on that treadmill recognize that San Diego is a place where our leisure options are nearly limitless and an obsessive commitment to leisure is recognized as normal. If we are to have strong leaders in San Diego, they will have to be able to play with the best of them.

Take a look outside. The climate is perfect, the sky compelling, the breeze gentle and the evenings cool. There is an undeniable lure to be outside in San Diego while the rest of the country huddles in front of the television with a bag of potato chips.

Laid Back

Decades ago, when the Beach Boys sang of shooting the curl, surfing, skateboarding and music became intertwined to create a California illusion that many in San Diego are still trying to live out. "Everybody's gone surfin'," may be lyric of fantasy to the rest of the landlocked country, but to anyone trying to get a hold of a building contractor, a pool man or a plumber, it's a grim reality. We are probably the only city on earth that actually boasts a company called, "Not When The Surf's Up Contractors."

Now, when you go to one of the great surfing beaches, the kids have to get out of the way of the 30- and 40-year-olds who are catching their daily waves. Mike Hynson was a 22-year-old in 1964 when the low budget movie, "The Endless Summer" featured his surfing. The movie grossed more than $30 million and he's still shaping boards at Windansea Beach 'n' Surf Shop in Pacific Beach. Larry Gordon and Floyd Smith started shaping surfboards in a garage in 1956. Today "Gordon and Smith" is a worldwide business, making surfboards, skateboards and designing leisurewear on computers for all of us who still want to play. San Diegans just want to have fun. And make money at it.

And we are having more fun, in more different ways, than anyone else. Not only have the traditional sports of golf and tennis done well here, and the typical water sports of surfing, sailing and sportfishing, we also have a abundance of specialized, off-beat leisure activities. Hang-gliding, jet-skiing, windsurfing, parasailing, roller blading, crewing, sand-castle-building and bungee-jumping are part of the leisure culture here, not to mention our infamous sport of Over-the-Line. We're talking serious leisure.

Because the last 20 years of leisure time has been coupled with another driving force that serves to provide a rationalization for our time outdoors – fitness. We now have the motivation that we need to have fun, be outdoors, take our sports seriously and spend lots of time playing. If we stop, we'll die. If we don't keep our bodies moving, we'll fall apart. Or, worse, look bad in a bathing suit or cycle pants, which is grounds for deportation in San Diego.

Together, fitness and leisure have a powerful grip on all San Diegans. Leisure is now a major industry. You can no longer jog and play basketball in the same shoe. You have to have two pairs. They each cost $100.

As a town, we are apathetic about sports teams but have a tremendous love for individualized sport heroes – the lone triathlete, the crazed race car driver, the champion surfer.

So, here's another opportunity for entrepreneurs. The organization of this leisure/fitness obsession is in the hands of a few volunteer sports clubs with minor corporate sponsorship.

Perhaps because there is so much diversity, our city has not encouraged the types of industries that could identify San Diego as the leisure/fitness capital of the world. Why not build on the good image of The Golden Door and La Costa? This is where you come to get fit, to learn about wellness, to exercise, to have a personal trainer change your life. Come to us, we will train you and you will have fun. And you will return.

"Show me a good loser in professional sports and I'll show you an idiot. Show me a good sportsman and I'll show you a player I'm looking to trade."

– Leo Durocher

12

Who's On First?

San Diegans don't like teams much. In a country where some cities have fan loyalty so ingrained that stadiums are regularly sold out and season tickets are closely guarded properties that are fought over in divorce court and passed down for generations, San Diego is almost unique in its apathy. We have contests, entertainment, free giveaways and still the fans don't come. This season a Thursday Padre game was attended by fewer than 8,600 people. Parking was great.

It's not that we don't like sports. But we like doing them. Everybody is an athlete, so the appeal of watching others participate is not so keen. Tell a group of British rugby football fans that they, too, could be playing instead of eating, drinking and screaming, they would think you were crazy. Tell a group of San Diegans that they can play instead of watch, they say, "When's the game?" It's a whole different mentality.

Take Me Out to the Home Team

Add to that the fact that practically everybody here is from somewhere else. Most San Diego fans are loyal to the teams they grew up with. We have a tremendous conglomeration of people who will always be Bears fans, always love the Raiders or always cheer for the Giants. In fact, typical of the self-esteem deficiency in San Diego, we do like other people's teams. When we had the Super Bowl, we had to expand the seating to 56,000 and the stadium was packed. The All-Star game was a sell-out. San Diegans have a little bit of a Groucho Marx philosophy – If it's our team, it can't be that great to watch. Bring us somebody else's team, we beat down the door. Getting the outside teams to come has not been easy, however. That same, sold-out Super Bowl was touch and go.

When Roger was mayor, it seemed clear to him that the city need-ed a good jolt. What better way, he thought, to excite this city and boost an already optimistic public mood, than to bring the greatest spectacle of all time to San Diego – the Super Bowl. So, Roger called Charger-owner Gene Klein in early 1984 and asked what he thought. "Gee, I was just talking about this," said Klein, "and I didn't think the city would be interested." Roger said, "You bet we are!" and together they resolved to get a task force formed and get to work. Parma, Payne, Burgener – the names on the task force read like a Who's Who of San Diego. The Booster Club was back in session and out to bag a Super Bowl.

With the NFL owners' meeting just months away, the task force worked feverishly, bringing in consultants, broadening its member-ship, mobilizing the media, contacting the business community and getting the support of neighborhood groups. Everybody in town caught Super Bowl fever.

Finally the day arrived. The Potentates of the NFL were meeting in Washington, D.C. under security that would make the President envious. Humbled supplicants from over 30 cities in the United States gather in small groups in the hotel lobby. Each group would get only 12 minutes to make its pitch.

Just ahead of the San Diegans, the San Francisco group led by Supervisor Quinten Kopp went overtime. Dignified in all things, the

NFL owners followed the lead of the Raider's Al Davis and peppered Kopp with their dinner rolls until he shut up. Then it was our turn.

Roger gave the pep talk of his life. He and others showed a video, described the expanse of the stadium, showed how seating could be expanded, documented the available hotel rooms, extolled the sight-seeing wonders of our town and, best of all, reminded everyone of the great weather in January. The San Diego delegation was upbeat, professional and, most importantly, finished within the time limit.

They might as well have saved their breath. Oh, Gene Klein was gracious in spreading the praise to Roger and the other members of the task force. But the real story was more direct.

It was the wee hours of the next morning. After many ballots and many discussions, it was not clear where that Super Bowl would land. Gene Klein got to his feet. He circled the room and reminded every owner how many millions of dollars they had personally pocketed as a result of the record-breaking television contract that Klein had negotiated for them. He looked each of them, including Al Davis, in the eye and said, "You owe me." They did, of course, and San Diego got its one and very possibly its only Super Bowl as a result.

The Sports Arena Saga

Another hero of getting teams here was a Canadian named Graham who asked the City of San Diego for a lease on Pueblo land to build the San Diego Sports Arena. Graham promised to bring in all kinds of professional teams to play here and, over the years, he did.

He built the Sports Arena as cheaply as possible and ended up with a terribly noisy, poorly-designed facility that had a great lease.

The City of San Diego gets a small portion of the parking fees and no funds from revenue of the actual events there. For the last 15 years of the lease, the city gets no revenue at all from the Sports Arena except what they can glean from the Swap Meet.

Meanwhile, the professional sports teams in the area have come and gone. During the growth mode of the last twenty years there has been a segment of San Diego that says without basketball and hockey, we aren't really a city.   These people are married to the people that say without our own symphony, we are not a city.

Unfortunately, too many of the couples that think this way stay home, watch the sports channel and play CDs. And the criteria to determine what makes a major city has changed. If we build it, they will come and go.

Only some people don't know it. During the last decade, when downtown renovation got serious, the vision was formed of moving the Sports Arena to downtown. A site was chosen near the convergence of the trolley lines and the plan was proposed for the arena to be a part of the new city center. Investors quietly bought up the old hotels and warehouses in the neighborhoods, waiting for the boom to happen.

The Cooper Coup

Then along came Harry Cooper. Harry Cooper is a brilliant businessman who loves sports, loves San Diego, loves life. He is the perfect San Diego hero – the self-made entrepreneur that took risks that paid off. He stepped up to the plate and said, "I'll save the Sports Arena, give it to me." A thankful San Diego City Council breathed a sigh of relief and gave him the lease. But Harry had not been going to his politician lunches at Dobson's. He had not been a participant in the carefully constructed balancing act between the Centre City Development Corporation, downtown investors, the city's planning department and the people who get thousands of dollars to do feasibility studies repeatedly for our civic leaders. Harry was an outsider.

So Harry announced to the city, here's what I want to do. Let me build a new sports arena on my land in Sorrento Valley. It is far more central to the entire county than downtown. It is not a residential neighborhood, so we don't have to worry about noise. There is great parking everywhere for night-time events. If I build a new stadium I can practically guarantee a hockey team and probably a basketball team. I'll make money, you'll make money, we'll get to see great sports and we'll all have fun.

At first there was only stunned silence. Then there was a cacophony of objections. Ron Hahn suddenly announced that he had one driving passion, and that was to bring the Sports Arena to downtown. Well, Ron's passion had a price tag and he arranged to buy back Harry Cooper's lease for $14 million, promising to get the funding for his dream arena.

Only now it's one year later and the dream arena is still a dream. Cooper is making legal noises about the validity of Hahn's actions. With overcrowded jails, empty high-rises and stalled development projects, the idea of plunking millions into a facility that will create a huge white elephant along the waterfront south of the Convention Center is an idea whose time may have come and gone.

We are not a team town and never will be. Put that money into a sports training facility where people can come from all over the globe to improve their skills and become peak athletes, you might have something. Create a place where couch potato conventioneers can come to San Diego and in two afternoons learn to use a Stairmaster and operate a hang-glider or try surfing and you might even make money. Let Nautilus and Nike pay for it, because they'll get the benefit. Why not?

Meanwhile, we need to think differently about sports. Do we need an arena that will bring lots of people to games, or a media center for sports and other events like national conventions or championship games? A hockey game doesn't attract 15,000 people, it attracts a worldwide audience. Reduce the number of seats and increase the number of box seats to keep your sophisticated team supporters, concert-goers and event-watchers. Let teams from everywhere else come here and play their hearts out. A worldwide audience is at stake here. Why not beam it up and see who salutes?

Going for Broke

This is the type of thinking that is rejuvenating the Del Mar Racetrack. The new facilities, which have been in the works for the past 20 years, contain the most successful and sophisticated intertrack wagering facilities in the state. The racing season in San Diego is now year-round, as patrons can relax, have lunch, place wagers and watch the actual races take place on satellite television. The new Turf Club includes more party rooms and a row of corporate boxes have been added.

In the meantime, while San Diegans are not sure what kind of entertainment developments to pursue, Tijuana has announced that it will build an amusement park, a roller coaster, a 148-acre theme park and will begin an earnest marketing effort to attract tourist trade. When the Disney company wanted to approach San Diego about moving its revered Anaheim park to our city, Maureen O'Connor refused to even meet with the Disney representatives. It may or may not have had something to do with the fact that she owns a hotel in Anaheim. Disney finally decided to expand there rather than relocate.

All change in San Diego has been the result of conscious government leadership encouraging and quietly subsidizing the individual entrepreneur. Harry Cooper was the entrepreneur without the support of government leadership. Ron Hahn is supported by politicians, but can't muster the subsidy. And as for sports teams filling up the stadiums? We couldn't even fill up a chapter without losing interest.

"Whenever a man does a thoroughly stupid thing it is always from the noblest motives."

– Oscar Wilde

13

"Buddy, Can You Spare a Dime?"

Helping needy people has always been a personal responsibility and a private charitable goal. Overwhelmed by the misery produced in the Great Depression, San Diego leaders looked to the government for a way to care for our citizens. Sixty years later, this is no longer an emergency measure for some, but a habit for too many.

The Department of Social Services in the County of San Diego is the largest department, by far, than any other agency. More than half of all County employees are under Social Services. It includes Child Protective Services and Aid to Families with Dependent Children (AFDC), which alone accounts for more than $525 million dollars in expenditures last year. And, although nearly 96 cents of every dollar in this department comes from state and federal funding, it is still a huge department and a huge responsibility for the County Board of Supervisors to supervise.

Child Protective Services

This arm of Social Services has grown dramatically in the last dozen years in response to legitimate community concerns about child abuse. The social workers were mandated from the beginning to prevent child abuse, to intervene, to assist families that were having real problems, to provide counseling, health care, parenting training and many other things beyond material support. The idea was to give whatever was needed to support parents to correct their problems and, if it did not work, to place the children in foster homes to prevent abuse or neglect. Adoption was a last resort.

From this most noble of motives has evolved the most corrupt county function ever to be encountered. Child Protective Services has completely overturned our legal system that requires all people to be considered innocent until proven guilty. It has ignored evidence that can restore families and actively works with the courts, not to develop the truth but to build evidence for abuse convictions.

How does this process work? Based on a single anonymous phone call, any child, anywhere, is automatically taken from the home. Originally, the system was designed to remove the child as rapidly as possible from a threatening situation. But the automatic nature of the policy has bypassed any guarantees that common sense will prevail.

On the flimsiest of calls made for whatever reason – an unhappy neighbor, a teacher with concerns, a bruise produced by a legitimate blood condition – the child is removed from the home by overworked, underpaid case workers who see ugly child abuse all day long and don't want to even deal with the validity of the complaint on any level.

In recent months the *Daily Californian* and *The San Diego Union-Tribune* printed stories about cases where this policy led to serious mistakes. A Navy father was accused of sexually molesting his four-year-old daughter. The child was not only removed from the home for three years, but was nearly adopted out to another family.

Were it not for a case of bureaucratic bungling, the child would have been adopted before the police and the social workers finally got together and discussed the fact that the semen on the little girl's panties did not match the father's. This was evidence that the police had from day one that the social workers never bothered to test. It turned out that the semen *did* match the semen found in other attacks in the same apartment complex, where another man had been charged with child molestation. These simple facts had never been linked by the investigators.

This family went through three years of hell. You can imagine what it was like for that father to go to work, for the mother to go shopping, for the other kids in the family and, most of all, for the little four-year-old girl who was in a foster home being told to admit that her father was the attacker. When confronted with these cases, the bureaucracy stonewalls, lies and denies. "This is an on-going case, we can't talk about it." "I don't recognize those facts." "This case is in court, we have no comment." The director of Social Services at the time, Jake Jacobson, who started out as a very bright, upcoming leader, reacted like the classic bureaucrat. "These are the disgruntled few. We have made no mistakes. There are no mistakes."

But there is a group called Victims of Child Protective Services and the members are filled with horror stories. Of course, there are those who are abusive and hiding behind the victim stance. But when you hear the number of cases and the evidence of error, it becomes pretty obvious that dozens of mistakes have been made. A significant number of people have been railroaded and abused by the social workers, police, psychiatrists, juvenile judges and the system as a whole. But no one is watching.

Who is in charge? Legally, the Board of Supervisors provides the accountability function for any County agency that is called into question. But what really happens is this. The bureaucrats say to the politicians, If we make one mistake in one thousand, then we've saved 999. Moreover, if you start attacking us, you are attacking your own program and you look bad. So the politicians, instead of being watchdogs, become mouthpieces for the bureaucrats.

This is not the civics you learned about in junior high.

Finally, in 1991, the evidence of misuse became overwhelming. There were stories about social workers who were taking kickbacks to direct certain adoptions. There were stories of social workers who think all men are evil and automatically guilty. There were stories of social workers who automatically condemn certain racial groups. There was the story of a social worker who was directing the adoption of a child, removed from the family on very flimsy evidence, and the adoptive parent was the social worker's sister.

This system was out of control. What we are talking about is criminal activity, malfeasance, the breaking up of the family by the government, all under the noble name of child protection.

Finally the Grand Jury acted and Jake Jacobson was removed. In October, the interim director, Cecil Steppe, held a press conference to announce that there would be a new wind blowing through Child Protective Services. The priority of the department was going to return to keeping families intact, helping abusers repair their lives, guiding families together, to solve their problems. We'll see.

Welfare

At the same time of the Child Protective Services mess, there were rumblings in the huge welfare department that irregularities were regular. This was not new. For a long time there have been those who have known that the whole purpose of the welfare department was not to help people, but to dole out money. The more money they dole, the more clients they have, the more files they maintain, the more workers they need, the more money they have to dole. It is really welfare for the middle class bureaucrats who need job security and opportunities to create more management levels. Create-a-job by helping the poor.

So when the stories about welfare fraud first began to circulate, it was easy to write them off as simple mismanagement.

Then, a courageous man stepped forward. David Sossaman was a National City policeman who had been in three shoot-outs and who finally was injured in an accident at the end of a high-speed chase. He was retired on disability and had been working as a welfare investigator for the Department of Social Services for three years. Sossaman called Roger on his KSDO talk show and said he was confident that there was 40 to 60 percent fraud in AFDC and that he could prove it. This amounted to about $200 million dollars a year, or almost four times the county budget deficit. Roger said, "You've got my attention."

David launched into stories. First, he told of a benefits analyst who was a drug dealer. She put clients on welfare and had them use the welfare payments to pay her for drugs. In investigating that further, Sossaman sought the help of the El Cajon Police Department, but they declined. Every time we cooperate with your department, they explained, someone in your department warns the criminals before we get there.

Other investigators called Roger and talked about the cashing of food stamps and other abuses. For instance, illegal aliens often come here from Tijuana to give birth. This makes them eligible for welfare. After the birth, they move back to Tijuana and live comfortably. Thousands of welfare checks go to post office boxes in San Ysidro and are picked up each week by mothers living in Mexico.

Sossaman's stories did not go unheeded. There began a determined effort to discredit and fire him. Attempts at entrapment were made and threats were sent. Other investigators were afraid to come forward. Jake Jacobson was a guest on Roger's KSDO show and denied everything. But the Grand Jury started an investigation and their report told a different story. Their report documented the fraud and estimated it at $70 million per year at the very least. Another reason Jake Jacobson was removed as head of the department.

Even before the Grand Jury report, David Sossaman had talked the Department of Social Services into letting him do a surprise audit of the Oceanside office of AFDC. His audit uncovered 60% of the files with some type of fraud in them. Everywhere in the system was misrepresentation, either with a male in the home, additional income that was unreported, additional children or different combinations of children than reported. Everyone knew about it and no one wanted to talk about it.

So the Department of Social Services allowed Sossaman to investigate other offices, but warned them first that an audit would be conducted. Even so, he still found 40% fraud. Then he found a new problem. Missing files. Up to 6,000 missing files.

An overpayment specialist got involved and began to inquire. The department told the specialist that files were in the records unit or they were in transit or they were lost and new files were issued. There were all kinds of reasons why the missing files were missing. But the money still went out.

On September 15, 1992 Cecil Steppe, interim director of the Department of Social Services, held a press conference and announced that all of the files were found. There were no more missing files. He invited Bonnie Kibbee, an East County activist, and Mark Miranda, another investigator, to come to his department and see for themselves.

Before they could go, another honest county employee called Bonnie and told her that they should look for the locked cabinet that had been removed to the office of a senior administrator. So Kibbee and Miranda went to the office, found the cabinet, had it opened and found 100 more files that fraud investigators had been seeking for weeks and months.

Here was real evidence of a cover-up of welfare fraud. This revelation made the new Grand Jury was even more upset than the first one. They saw that the department had no credibility whatsoever. They saw denial and cover-up. They saw David Sossaman threatened and unable to do his job and they saw the response of the department, which was, so what? We are following state and federal guidelines and you can't touch us. It's federal money, anyway, what do you care?

But there is no "federal money." There is a federal deficit. And the interesting thing is that if you add it up, every county and every state in the United States, cutting fraud in welfare payouts by 40%, the total is nearly equal to the federal deficit.

In other words, if we were only helping the truly needy, we would have a more balanced federal budget and no new taxes.

Wake Up the Watchdogs

The Board of Supervisors does have both the responsibility and the authority to regulate the actions of the Department of Social Services, even if most of the money comes from the federal and state governments. If County employees are violating their offices, it is the local elected officials who must demand accountability.

The victims can't do it all. Although they are certainly bringing lawsuits against CPS, for instance, the County always settles. In fact, the county seems to want to be sued, because then the CPS victims are paid off by other taxpayers. There is no sanction against their own actions or their own department or against their own budget. Every lawsuit has a clause that requires the plaintiffs to keep quiet and not disclose the terms of the settlement. So the choice is to talk about it out loud and get nothing, or take the money and stay quiet. It's a pay-off, pure and simple. With your money.

What this whole fiasco has proven is that the elected officials have lost control and the bureaucracy is running its own agenda at our expense. Public officials are not making these administrators responsible and it is taking strong public opinion to create action.

Who's In Charge Here?

Here's proof that the bureaucracy of San Diego government is powerful. We had just witnessed concern over the fact that the City of San Diego was facing a budget crisis. The city was going to lose $30 million. The total budget was $1 billion.

But the "loss" was not a deduction from last year's total. It was a loss of $30 million from next year's projected (and expected) increase. It was a debate about how much the budget could not increase, not how much would have to be cut.

It was the same in the state crisis. California was without a budget for 64 days in 1992. Last year they spent $56 billion and change. But for all the crying and stalemating and problems and IOU's, the fight was not over cuts, but increases. The budget as passed for 1993 is still over $57 billion. So why are they talking cutbacks?

Every private business has had to streamline over the past few years. People are not talking about increases. They are talking about frozen salaries, hiring freezes and making cuts.

But the state bureaucracy is so powerful that they have convinced people that services need to be cut to balance the budget. This is simple punishment to the taxpayer.

Public school bureaucrats tell the public with a straight face, for instance, that they need more money even though they are using less than half of school money in the classroom. We say, put the money you already have back in the classroom and then ask for more if you really need it.

114

Probably every California taxpayer is under the impression that because of Proposition 13, schools have less money. But this is not true. Property tax revenues in the City of San Diego are more than 250% of what they were in 1978. Houses have sold and more have been built. There has been an incredible increase in revenue.

Furthermore, the county budget went from $485 million in 1978 to $2 billion today. Even with population growth, that is a massive bureaucratic explosion. You can't account for a government that big. They added reams of lawyers, reams of consultants, reams of clerks, but have reduced the number of policemen per thousand in San Diego since 1987. The intent of the bureaucracy is to threaten the taxpayer and punish him for daring to suggest that other areas be cut.

And, if you think for a moment that the elected officials are in charge, look at the sworn testimony in the Bray-Spaulding sexual harassment court case. There, former City Manager John Lockwood said he did not tell the City Council about the $100,000 payoff to Bray for her silence because, "the Council could not keep a secret!!!"

This bureaucracy is one of the key reasons why San Diego is having difficulty painting its next future and having a clear vision of our next destiny. Thousands of public employees are trying to protect their turf and they are incapable of innovation. Whatever the next agenda for prosperity requires, we may find ourselves unable to accomplish it because of this bureaucratic monster that demands to be fed.

David Sossaman is on unpaid, administrative leave. Although he has been a courageous citizen, and honest employee and a persever-

115

ing investigator, the bureaucrats have promised him his career is over.

He has already been interviewed by Dianne Sawyer and Dan Rather. The Welfare Fraud Scandal in San Diego is now national news. But the fact is, any employee that tries to right the injustices of bureaucracy must pay the price. That is why the duty belongs with our elected officials.

Susan Golding has written to the California Department of Social Services asking for a complete audit. This story is not over and the fraud is far from ended. It's time for people to wake up and understand that elected officials are not acting in their best interests, but are in bed with bureaucrats and sleeping with the status quo. Only the conscious, determined demands of active citizens will break them up.

If we ignore it, it will engulf us.

"We live under a government of men and morning newspapers."

– Wendell Phillips

14

Media and Politics

You Read It Here First

Here in San Diego, as elsewhere in the world, the media has become much more than the messenger. But the difference here in San Diego is that it has been that way for a very long time. As in other towns, our hometown newspaper has set the agenda, decided who's hot and who's not and has been one of the town's power brokers. Nowhere else has that power been more tightly held than here by *The San Diego Union/Tribune.*

To be sure there have been and are now many other voices. *The San Diego Sun* and the *San Diego Independent* were past efforts to compete with the *San Diego Union.* But in reality, the *San Diego Union* and *San Diego Tribune*, now co-mingled, have dominated the social, cultural and political life of this region virtually since the Civil War.

Some of that has to do with its politics. Founded by a Union Civil War veteran in a Republican city full of Union veterans, there was little opposition to the message of the newspaper for long, long time. For all its modern diversity, San Diego to this day is essentially a Republican town.

Some of the power also has to do with the past leadership of the newspaper. Back in the '50s and '60s, when Jim Copley owned the paper and C. Arnholt Smith owned the politics, the *San Diego Union* had no rival for information. Fledgling television operations read the *Union* to find out what to cover, to decide what was news.

Harold Keen, a brilliant writer and opinionated Democrat, reported for Channel 8 and hosted San Diego's first interview show that gave

118

political figures an independent platform to spread their views. Keen also wrote for years for *San Diego Magazine* in a trend that continues today. Many of the city's best writers can't, or won't write for the *Union*.

But the leadership that gave the *San Diego Union* such power is the same element with diminished power today. With the death of Jim Copley and Smith's prosecution and downfall, the beginning of the end began. And the end of the end is near.

Helen Copley, who was Jim's secretary and later his second wife, inherited control of the Copley Newspapers empire. Her stake at its peak value in the mid-'80s was estimated at more than $850 million.

But Helen was not prepared to be the boss. A shy, very private person, Helen Copley is shrewd, but not intelligent. Driven, but not principled, she has relied on Jim's old cronies and her close circle of fiercely loyal friends to maintain a facade of confidence and the appearance of competence. She still does.

Roger, Meet Helen

Roger met Helen Copley for the first time in 1975. As a young lawyer with Higgs, Fletcher and Mack, Roger was considering running against incumbent County Supervisor Lou Conde, a nut case whose antics caused private laughter, but whose right-wing advocates were thought so powerful that no more-well-known challengers were willing to step forward.

Pete Wilson offered to do the introduction. Pete and Roger traveled to one of those wonderful downtown pre-redevelopment Chinese restaurants and were seated at a large round table opposite Helen, who sat in the corner surveying the room. She had little to say during lunch, while others, including Herb Klein and Neil Morgan, kept the conversation going. Finally, Pete Wilson stated the case for Roger's challenge and indicated that he should speak on his own behalf.

Roger geared up. He began what he hoped would be a clear and compelling speech on his vision for the future of San Diego County. But about 20 seconds into it, Mrs. Copley interrupted him with an abrupt question. "Is this the race that Bill Mitchell is running in?" she asked. Helen was assured that yes, Bill Mitchell, a La Jolla realtor, was another of the primary election challengers.

She then asked a second question, "Isn't he the realtor who tried to sell my son David **that** house?"

With that, the topic was closed. Roger received the *San Diego Union's* editorial support for the first and last time, presumably because he had not tried to sell David Copley anything inappropriate.

Roger's next encounter with Helen Copley happened, at his request, in her office at the *Union/Tribune* building in Mission Valley in 1982. Roger, now one of the County supervisors, was making the rounds, feeling out the potential support for a run at the mayoral seat, should Pete Wilson be successful at beating Jerry Brown for the U.S. Senate.

Again, about 20 seconds into his pitch, Helen interrupted him. "Why did you vote against Ram's Hill?" she asked. It took Roger several awful moments to make sense of the question. Then he remem-

120

bered the Borrego Springs project. Roger had held up the project when it was discovered the developer was planning to dump the sewage from the homes into the same groundwater being proposed to provide drinking water. Roger had acted to halt the project until an alternative sewage disposal plan was in place.

Roger started to explain his reasoning when Helen fixed him with a stare and said, slowly, "Didn't you know that project was next to my Rancho Zorro?" That was the end of the conversation.

Thus, Roger's vote, which somehow affected Copley real estate interests in Borrego Springs, determined for all time that he was on the outs. This and not all of the made-up chaff that appeared in subsequent Copley editorials during the mayoral campaign, determined which candidate would be endorsed. The meeting was over.

Helen Copley fought fiercely for the election of her friend Maureen O'Connor in that 1983 special election. On the editorial pages and in the news pages as well, O'Connor's election was treated as a natural force, a logical certainty. Unfortunately for Roger Hedgecock, he was elected instead. He was the first San Diego mayor ever to win without the support of the *San Diego Union*.

Helen Copley never forgot. Even after the trial, even after the conviction, Copley could not forget. Four years after Roger began his show on KSDO, Helen Copley ran into the chief executive officer of the Gannett Corporation at a national publishers' convention.

Gannett is better known for owning *USA Today* and 214 newspapers than it is for owning radio stations. But it does own about a dozen stations, including San Diego's KSDO. Copley approached Gannett's

CEO with a request: Fire Roger Hedgecock at KSDO. The Gannett chief, John Curley, was somewhat taken aback by this direct appeal. He declined to honor Mrs. Copley's "request" and told her she should take the matter up with the General Manager of KSDO, who had full authority over hiring and firing any employee. The only thing she accomplished was to make the head of Gannett aware of Roger!

The Editorial Vote

This is the way influence works in San Diego. Early in Roger's tenure as mayor, he was sitting in his office when the telephone rang and the last of the bank of phone number extensions lit up. Always before the first line had rung. The remaining three lines were reserved for rollover calls and for calling out. For this line to ring, it had to be deliberately called not to go through the office. Roger's secretary answered the call anyway and announced Ed Fike, editorial editor of the *San Diego Union*.

"Hello, Ed," said Roger, "Is there some reason that you dialed this number?" "I always use this number so I can call the mayor directly," explained Fike. He went on to instruct Roger on the Copley position concerning an agenda item that was coming up before the City Council and solicited his support.

"Thank you," said Roger. "I'll consider your position." Which he did. And he disagreed. Then he voted his mind and never heard from Ed Fike on the private line to the mayor's office again.

On the Other Hand

The Daily Californian in East County is one of several daily newspapers that is trying to make a living as an alternative to the *San Diego
Union*. As a regional paper, it services nine communities with four dis-
tinct cities and seventeen school districts, which makes for lots of city
council squabbles, school board politics and County government concern.

The other regional daily newspapers – the *Times/Advocate* in
North County, the *Blade/Citizen* in North Coastal and the *Star News
South* in South Bay – join *The Daily Californian* in daily struggle to
wrest advertising not only from the metropolitan giant but from the
hundreds of other weekly community papers that have come into
being because San Diego readers are so hungry for localized and unbi-
ased reporting. It makes for very hungry publishers.

Francine first met Paul Zindell, publisher of *The Daily Californian*,
in her fourth interview for the position of managing editor. She had
spent over 20 hours talking to staff on both the news and advertising
sides of the operation, each one skeptical of her desire and ability to
take on the job. She would be the fourth editor in two years. One had
lasted less than two weeks.

In that interview, Francine laid out her position on the role of an
editor for a community paper and the publisher seemed pleased. "We
want you to have complete freedom," he said. "Of course, we don't
want to hang the mayor, but we want you to be autonomous."

Francine's first thought was, Helen Copley hung the mayor.

123

Knowing what a fiasco that had been for the San Diego, Francine vowed to herself that she would put the truth above politics as editor.

So when the eager and brilliant reporter, Mike Drummond, was set to do a story on the homeless in East County, there was no hesitation. And when Mike Drummond discovered that he could interview the homeless son of El Cajon Mayor, Joan Shoemaker, there was still no hesitation. The interview was powerful, with Shoemaker revealing many details of life with his step-father and his mother. He told many painful and private stories.

But the focus of the story was homelessness, and Shoemaker's story was a sidebar. The purpose of including it was to illustrate that homeless situations can arise from any family background, any family setting. The sidebar was kept brief.

As a courtesy to Joan, Francine called her on Christmas Eve, the night before the story would run. "I want you to know, Joan," said Francine, "we are not using this story to embarrass you in any way. We are not printing any private details. Mother to mother, we can hope that this story will create action that will help those who need help."

But editor to mayor, Francine had forgotten to be political. Joan had voted against nearly every project to help the homeless that had run across her desk. By the end of December 26th, Francine had been called a liar and had made an enemy.

And in the same way that a publisher and a mayor at odds can be damaging to the truth, a publisher and a mayor in cahoots undermines integrity. A few months later Mike Drummond wrote two stories about

El Cajon that appeared on the same Sunday front page – a business was moving out of the downtown redevelopment district and a group of teenage runaways were discovered living in the drain pipes underneath El Cajon. The first was a simple story of a disgruntled business-owner. The second was a sensitive and moving tale describing how these youngsters had created a "family" with a shared sense of responsibility and accountability to each other. Mayor Joan was livid.

Never once did she talk to Francine. Joan faxed the publisher in New York expressing her dismay at the articles, which put El Cajon in a "negative" light. Paul, instead of backing up his staff like John Curley had done with Roger, denounced Drummond and criticized the coverage. Francine refused to reprimand the reporter and offered her resignation.

Paul arrived Monday morning and accepted the resignation without pause. He had already hired editor number five, Jim Schumacher, who was a childhood friend from New York. "I wasn't going to fire you, Francine," Paul said. "I was going to have Jim do it."

Mike Drummond was fired the following week as he returned from his honeymoon, in the parking lot on a Sunday afternoon. He was refused access to the building. Later his story won a top award from the San Diego Press Club.

Keep It Separate

The point of these stories is really the same. Media and politics belong in separate camps. When the mayor can fire the editor or when the publisher can fire the mayor, we all lose. And just as we need to be careful watchdogs of our elected officials, we also need to be watchdogs of the press. You can't believe everything you read in the paper, folks. Check the facts in the small regional papers that are tremendously dependent on advertising dollars and the good will of the community leaders. And check the facts of the over-bloated metropolitan papers that are dependent on the personal whims of the publisher. Either way, there is another agenda going on.

Decide For Yourself

Thankfully, diversity in San Diego media is on the rise. Television is more independent, competent and confident as the primary news source for a majority of San Diegans. KSDO and other news radio organizations have, likewise, forged an independent path by reporting the news as they see it. Community newspapers, *The Reader*, the *San Diego Business Journal*, and the *Daily Transcript*, are providing alternative views.

Unheard of 15 years ago, the *San Diego Union* editorial endorsements in the last San Diego City Council elections were all defeated. Is the *Union/Tribune* support now the kiss of death? What a turnaround.

As a merged newspaper, the *Union/Tribune* is smaller and not as cocky, but still cranky. Its editorials pursue issues such as the airport location and NAFTA that are against the popular will. With no cohesive booster group to rally popular support, the paper sounds like a lonely, off-key trumpet in an orchestra pit where the rest of the players have gone home.

Helen Copley may be tired of the ordeal. Her son David's heart attack a year ago has ended forever any illusions that he will pull together the reins of power and take charge of the enterprise. Direct mail's successful attack against newspaper advertising has left all print media weakened. The *Union/Tribune's* circulation is less than 25% of the population of San Diego County, a pitiful penetration for a metropolitan newspaper. Without the trust of the public, without the belief that the paper is a source for truth, there really is no point to it. And who has the time?

Flawed as it may be, the time is near when television news will become the major source of daily news in this country. Sound facts from *USA Today* and thought-bite evaluations in *Time* and *Newsweek*. Computer news services are already available and personal subscribers to these services are able to circumvent newspapers altogether and evaluate the news for themselves.

But there will always need to be a watchdog. There will always need to be a trust in the news-source, whether it comes from the printed page, the radio or the modem. Integrity and ethics, qualities that we now associate with good journalism, will be needed more than ever as our news sources expand. That is where you, the reader, the listener, the viewer, has to participate, question, and evaluate where the truth may be found. And then decide what to believe.

If you swallow it whole, you deserve the bellyache.

"The marvel of all history is the patience with which men and women submit to burdens unnecessarily laid upon them by their government."

– William E. Borah

15

Politics and Politics

Politics in San Diego looks corrupt. With more than a surface glance, however, you discover that politics in San Diego is simply so diffused that it seems terminally unable to get anything whatsoever done.

Not that the people are incompetent. Many fine people run for office here and many fine people are elected to school boards, city councils, even the Board of Supervisors. But the institutions of local government were designed for ineffectiveness, in an era when ineffectiveness was a virtue. Let us explain.

They Don't Know How

San Diego's exploding population and an even more exploding expectation of the role of government has caused local government to fail. There is simply not the sophistication and knowledge necessary to administer a myriad of multi-billion dollar programs that are now needed to run our county. Politicians themselves don't have much power, they don't know what to do with it when they get it and are content to let the bureaucrats tell them what to do with it anyway. Elected officials may come and go, but top staff positions remain the same. Or, even if the actual person changes, the mentality behind the position never wavers.

The city charter for San Diego was enacted in 1931 by an outraged citizenry because of overt corruption. There had been a strong mayor and a strong City Council which hired and fired not only the city manager but also each other's various uncles and others to do all of the public works for the city.

When the progressive area of American politics hit San Diego, it reinstated a higher purpose for public office, including serving the public good. This revision allowed, for a few brief decades, Americans to think that burgeoning government taxes, under government control, might be a good thing for the citizens.

This notion built into the city charter the role of the City Council as a policy-making body, with no authority to hire or fire anybody. It was a part-time group that would decide the broad outlines of city policy and leave the day-to-day matters to the city manager.

The city manager, under this charter, was given the power to prepare budgets, hire, fire, provide information to elected officials and to make recommendations on all matters. The mayor was reduced to being merely one of nine people on the City Council, with a single line on the charter giving the mayor the power to conduct meetings. The charter of 1931 remains in effect to this day.

But typical of San Diego, strong mayors have always been elected. The mayor is the single most visible representative of the city. A strong-willed mayor has always been able to make things happen in San Diego, even though he has had absolutely no power to do so under the city charter. Here is where the need for a strong individual with a vision to create San Diego has been true 100% of the time.

Strong mayors have consistently left their stamp on the city. Mayor Dale, in the 1960s inspired the formation of a downtown business group that began the effort to create the community concourse during the late Frank Curran's term. A more recent example was the determination of Pete Wilson to use state law to create authority for himself apart from the city manager. The key was the new concept of planning.

Wilson at the Helm

California law required the adoption of a city plan during Wilson's tenure and city councils were required to be the policy-making bodies for the plan. Wilson put these two requirements together and created a planning department under the authority of the City Council, not the city manager. Then he created the Centre City Development Corporation (CCDC) to carry out the mandates of another state law which required each City Council to develop or act as a redevelopment board. Wilson succeeded in creating a parallel bureaucracy to the city manager's bureaucracy that would answer to him. He then took the Comprehensive Planning Organization, a volunteer group that represented the various cities throughout the county, and decided that long-range planning was also a state requirement under his authority. Through sheer force of personality, he dominated the CPO, which later became SANDAG, and limited the authority of the county government as well. The priority of planning allowed him to leapfrog over all the existing authority and to drive city policy toward his own goals. Wilson became a very powerful mayor as a result.

Wilson took advantage of weak city managers during his tenure, and replaced them with his own. He also used election laws to control City Council members. Each council member had to be nominated in their district, but elected in a citywide race six weeks later. Wilson went about systematically influencing the narrow base of political contributors – mostly developers, savings & loan institutions and insurance companies – to support those candidates that would work with him. For instance, Maureen O'Connor was never number one in her council district, but gained office through a city-wide election with Wilson's endorsement and favors.

Next Wilson created the committee system in the City Council. He made council members full time employees, with pay. All committee agendas were given out by the rules committee and the chairman of the rules committee was the mayor. Now Wilson had more power than any other mayor before him. Nothing could come before the City Council that he had not allowed. The city manager was cut off and Wilson controlled the agenda.

In 1973, Pete Wilson proposed amendments to the city charter that would separate the mayor from the council members and set up the classic U.S. model of executive and legislative checks and balances. It was overwhelmingly defeated by the voters who had no idea that what they had actually rejected was, in fact, already in place at City Hall.

What Have We Got Now?

Today, these sweeping changes have largely been reversed. The committee system has been changed so that any member of the council can bring any matter to any committee. The city manager has placed a staff person on each council committee to set the agenda.

So the current system took power back to the city manager and the power that Pete Wilson carefully accumulated over a dozen years is gone from the mayor's office. But his proposal for district elections finally passed on the fourth go-round.

However, district elections without separation of the mayor's office has resulted in a totally gridlocked City Council. Today the council can't do anything. It has nine mayors. And the most recent mayor only exercised her power in the negative. She could stop anything, but she couldn't get anything done.

These days the San Diego City Council is on the defensive. There is no clear leadership. The Council has become very good at allowing the city to run out of control. The planning department has an increase in personnel even though they have less work to do. The attorneys are completely out of control, with dozens and dozens of them doing less work all the time. There is no one at the helm and the ship is lurching across uncharted waters with no idea where it's going. The city staff who manage the sails are simply maintaining minimum rigging and hoping that somebody, somewhere, will grab the tiller.

At this point in our history, the mayor cannot direct the bureaucracy. That single fact is keeping us from solving the old problems of the airport, land use, sewage and more. Even more devastating is that new opportunities are falling on deaf ears as well. The proposals by Disney, the proposal to set up the automobile port of entry, the Defense Department proposal that would create 7,000 jobs – these are slipping away. The authority in the city has become so diffused, so out of control that there is no way to get anything done.

Recently the San Diego chief of police released statistics that violent crime was up for the third year in a row. No one on the City Council had the nerve to hold him accountable. No one had the nerve to say, why are you still here? What would it take? Would violent crime have to go up, say 25% percent to get a new chief? Would it have to climb 30%? Would it have to climb 50%? Is there any point at all at which the City Council can say to the chief of police, "You're fired!" Nobody wants to rock the boat because nobody wants to fall out. Members of the City Council have one purpose and that is to be re-elected as members of the City Council.

Let's take the example of homeless people downtown. Everybody is concerned about this problem. Some people find that just the sight and smell of these homeless are offensive. Tourists are offended by the panhandling. Business owners are horrified to come to work and find someone sleeping in his own feces at the doorstep. Everyone agrees that something needs to be done.

The problem is this: Most of these problems are happening in the city, but Social Services is handled by the county. The city and the county are not talking to each other, so no solutions are forthcoming.

So the city put bandages on the issue by creating bathrooms and emergency shelters. But the city attorney said, We can't waste the time of the police on this, we have other priorities. Social services said, We have run out of free beds. The courts said, It is not a crime to be homeless. Finally, after you have exhausted all of these avenues, the homeless are still on the street and the public is still upset.

One person made a difference. It took a strong individual from the private sector, Father Joe Carroll, to come to grips with this problem. And not only to come to grips with it but to deal with the nuances like clothing, job training, school for the homeless children, rental deposits for people living in their cars. And the spectacle of a single person declaring that he could and would do something about the homeless situation that saw the bureaucracy at a standstill has been rewarded, with an outpouring of private money.

And the bureaucracy has never been able to forgive him for being successful. As the Joan Kroc/St. Vincent de Paul Center has continued to expand and more beds are added, the city has not responded in kind. Recently Father Joe Carroll has been assessed $130,000 in city permit fees, which could have been waived by the City Council. So a huge portion of private money, raised to solve the homeless problem that the city is unable and unwilling to handle, goes back to city coffers as a hidden tax.

Ring Out the Old, Ring In the New

As a nation, we have come to an end of the Cold War. As a region, business and industry are transforming. Defense manufacturing is a setting sun after a brilliant day. In the wake of the savings & loan crisis, local titans like Kim Fletcher and Gordon Luce are fallen. In the mayoral election of 1992, an outsider, neophyte Peter Navarro very nearly won out against the inside, experienced politician Susan Golding. The Board of Supervisors, shaken by budget mismanagement, the CPS scandal and the welfare fraud revelations has gotten two new members and more will be ousted.

Our political structures have changed. Traditionally, developers and allied suppliers, financiers and the building trades would fuel the campaigns of like-minded, growth-oriented office-seekers. These folks are broke, gone. The business community in a branch town like San Diego does not have the money to wield the clout that can be wielded in headquarters towns like L.A. and Dallas. Meanwhile, the campaigns are getting more and more expensive while the sources of campaign money are drying up. And not just because of the recession.

But, right or wrong, all this reminds us how San Diego was built. Against all the odds, against all opposition, against all the dirty tricks and the back-stabbing, we have had new heroes come forward to say, This is what needs to be done, follow me and we will do it. Financing these changes are small business leaders, professional people and community activists who have suddenly found that they are powerful and have begun to operate in networks of grass roots campaigns.

Now, more than ever, San Diego is, at once, both a closed, large, small-town and a wide-open opportunity for determined leadership. Bright, young newcomers are running for local offices.

The democratic spirit has not died in San Diego. The "can-do" spirit has not died. More and more people are recognizing what needs to be done and are willing to step forward to do it. The last 50 years of government over-promises are over. There is no one left who believes that the government will fulfill all its missions and people are mad as hell.

The next item on the agenda is to get free from a government bureaucracy that we have allowed to get too big and too expensive and too intrusive. New Congress members, Assembly members and State Senators will need a period of orientation – a far cry from 20 years ago when all was decided in advance from the set ranks of pre-designated-candidates drawn from the Elks Club or the Downtown Rotary. Private coalitions are forming. Power shifts are taking place.

Some elected officials have gotten the message loud and clear that they work for the public, not the staff. A hurricane of change can be seen on the horizon that will propel San Diego into the next century with solutions, not only to the old problems, but to the new and complex issues that will be confronting us in the next ten years. Let it come.

CONCLUSION

Do You Get the Picture?

San Diego is an ever-changing, interacting mosaic of individual efforts, of individual triumphs and defeats – a town invented, torn down and re-invented by determined spirits from all over the world and with all points of view. In other words, we are poised to become the proto-typical 21st Century city. Just as we have always been a perfect test-market for every product that comes down the pike, so we are the test-market for a new politic, a new way of doing business, a new way of educating ourselves, entertaining ourselves, training ourselves. We are the test market for the future.

San Diego needs **more** interaction, **more** diversity and yes, **more** persistence from each of us, to really work. The advantage that we have over other cities is that it has always been that way here. There's a long tradition of successful re-invention and now that spirit is needed more than ever. Your involvement in crucial to this enterprise. Your persistence will pay off. A new San Diego is waiting to be defined, inspired and created by you.

If we say it enough, we'll believe it – and make it happen.

``*A hero is no braver than an ordinary man, but he is brave five minutes longer.*"

– R. W. Emerson